Dream Interpretation for Better Sleep

Find Meaning in the Messages of your Subconscious Mind to Build your own Dream Dictionary

JOANNE HEDGER

Dear Reader

Like so many people, I would cringe when I arrived at work in the morning to be greeted with a colleague uttering the dreaded words, "I had the strangest dream last night," because I knew politeness would make me endure the whole story of some fellow worker's race against a giant roll of sticky tape through the back alleys of a London borough and reaching the edge of a precipice before turning into a washing machine... blah blah blah. Other peoples' dreams used to bore the pants off me. That is until I discovered a way to decipher them and find the clear messages my own brain was generating for me.

There are many benefits to interpreting your dreams and few dangers, but we will explore both, along with step-by-step instructions for creating your personalized dream dictionary and finding meaning in the often-absurd scenarios played out by your night mind.

Undoubtedly, science has come a long way and many studies have been made about sleep and dreams. However, this book is not about science. It is about how I found the ability to understand what my inner brain is trying to tell me while I sleep and sharing that experience with you in the hope that you will be persuaded to do the same, or at the very least, give you pause for thought next time you wake up having remembered a dream.

Contents

"All that we see or seem is but a dream within a dream"
– Edgar Allen Poe

Introduction

This short read is for those who are tired of having the same dream over and over again and not being able to work out what it means. It's also for those who simply want to understand the basics of how to get started decoding their dreams.

What possible message could be hidden in that weird and wacky dream I had last night?

This is not a book of science or religion, nor is it a lengthy explanation of the theories of Freud and his friends. However, it is a well-known and widely held belief that your subconscious can provide deep insights into your true self. This is a practical book about how you can unlock those insights and take a fascinating journey towards a better understanding of how you perceive the world and how the world perceives you.

For me, the ability to decode my dreams has guided me for many years now. It has led me to make decisions and choices in life that have helped me grow as a person and ultimately become a happier one. We are the only ones who must live with our conscience; we are the only ones who can make ourselves happy. So, listening to your inner voice, your subconscious, played out while you sleep is a fascinating first step to take towards happiness. Through decoding my dreams, I have learned to listen to that inner voice, act, and as a result:

1) I no longer have disturbing dreams that repeat for weeks
2) I no longer find myself thinking, *I'll be happy when....*
3) I have the confidence to make brave decisions in life
4) I have a better understanding of my strengths and weaknesses and what I need to do about them

I will admit that often it is like playing a cryptic game of charades in your head or a frustrating puzzle that you struggle to solve. Thankfully, your mind is an astonishingly clever bit of kit and if the message is important enough, it will not give up trying to find ways for you to grasp the meaning or solve the puzzle. The moment that you crack it is an "aha" moment of huge delight.

Unlike other books about dreaming, this DIY method focuses largely on the process involved in completing it. It is not a generic dream dictionary; you will not find an index full of common themes, symbols, or objects found in dreams with a corresponding "meaning". There is a good reason for this which we will discuss later.

I am not a scientist, neuro or otherwise. I will admit I am fascinated by the unexplained within our brains and, over the years, I have read a fair number of books on the subject. Some of them I found fascinating while others were not worth the money I paid for them, and certainly not worth the time it took me to digest the science within. This book is short, concise and to the point. It aims to give you the tools you need to get started today.

Chapter 1

The Secrets of Sleep

Sleep means different things to different people. For some, it's a way for their mind and body to rest after a hard day's work. Others see it as an escape from reality; a chance to enter their own private world. It can even be a symptom of depression or other underlying health issues. To sleep is also to dream, and both are inextricably linked.

One thing we all have in common is the need to sleep a certain number of hours each night, and those hours should be undisturbed. We all have to lay our head down somewhere and catch some Zs in any 24-hour period and the lack of sleep can seriously affect our ability to function when awake.

We talk about sleep a lot and will often hear or say things like "I didn't sleep at all last night," "I slept badly," "I slept like a baby," or, "I can never get enough sleep." And our final wish for our loved ones at the end of each day is that they, "Sleep well...sweet dreams." It appears that our obsession with how well and how much we sleep makes up a big part of the narrative during our wakeful state.

The truth is that we all appreciate getting a deep, restful, bountiful sleep each night, and the younger we are, the more we need. New-born babies need up to 17 hours of sleep, which is a godsend for the exhausted parents. As grown adults, we require anywhere from 7 to 9 hours of sleep each night if we want to get through the day without having a meltdown of some sort.[1] But have you ever wondered why we need sleep at all?

It seems kind of weird to think that we leave ourselves exposed to dangers in such a

---

[1] Hirshkowitz, Max et al. "National Sleep Foundation's sleep time duration recommendations: methodology and results summary." *Sleep health* vol. 1,1 (2015): 40-43. doi:10.1016/j.sleh.2014.12.010

vulnerable state for long periods of time when we sleep, although we aren't the only animals to do so. Some species actually sleep way more than us, which just goes to show that even in the wild, the need for sleep outweighs any risks it might entail.

Depending on whether you are a three-toed sloth that needs 16 hours of sleep per day, a brown bat sleeping for 19.9 hours a day, or an African elephant snoozing for only 4 hours out of the full 24, sleep is still king – or queen! Sleep cycles may be different, depending on what species you are, how big your brain is, what you eat, your body mass index, social hierarchy, and other factors like genes, but we still do it in some shape or form. Dolphins are an intriguing case because only half of their brain sleeps at a time, and they can even continue to swim while asleep, which I personally find very impressive.

As humans, our sleep needs become monophasic when we mature (sleeping for one portion of time) or biphasic (napping during the day). Cats and dogs, on the other hand, can sleep on and off for short intervals throughout the 24-hour cycle, making them polyphasic. No matter how many legs you have, sleep is essential, and good quality sleep, or 'efficient' sleep, is paramount to our well-being for so many reasons.

Contrary to popular myth, we even sleep more now than our primal ancestors did, although we have seriously messed up our natural cycle. When researchers looked at the sleeping habits of traditional societies in Bolivia, Tanzania, and Namibia in a study carried out in 2015[2], they discovered something quite amazing. If these societies are any indication of what our hunter-gatherer forefathers used to live like, then we can see that they slept an average of 6.5 hours per night. That's below the recommended 7 hours minimum that we are told we need today by sleep experts.

---

[2] Natural Sleep and Its Seasonal Variations in Three Pre-industrial Societies - ScienceDirect, Current Biology Vol. 25, Issue 21, 2015

The difference is, though, that these traditional groups didn't delay sleep because they were watching late-night TV shows, swiping their mobile phones while in bed, or consuming large amounts of alcohol until the wee hours. They seemed to follow a pretty regular routine of going to sleep about 3.3 hours after sunset and waking up when the early morning temperature was at its lowest. They weren't known to take naps during the day and had no word in their vocabulary for 'insomnia' – one of the most common complaints of the western world today.

Led by UCLA professor of psychiatry and biobehavioural sciences, Dr Jerome Spiegel, the above study observed that no matter which continent they were on, both the African and South American subjects tended to wake just after daybreak, and all received maximum light exposure in the morning. We already know that morning light plays a crucial role in regulating mood and the neurons that manage the brain's internal clock, which is why exposure to it is a suggested treatment for those suffering from depression.

It seems like going against the day's natural ebb and flow can seriously affect our sleep quality and our health, especially when the time we go to bed has nothing to do with sunrise and sunset anymore. It's not surprising then that we put so much emphasis on trying to enjoy a 'good night's sleep' and are only too aware of the negative side effects if we can't achieve that.

We are only just beginning to understand what sleep is, why we need it, what keeps us from sleeping, and how sleep deprivation affects us. Thanks to advances in neuroscience, we can see what goes on in our brain throughout the sleep cycle and its quite powerful stuff. It's definitely about more than just having a rest after a long day. Sleep is essential for our survival!

What is sleep?

Broadly speaking, sleep is a state during which our awareness of environmental stimuli is reduced. That means we are totally oblivious to what is going on around us when snoozing although our brain is super-active at that time. We fall in and out of sleep thousands of times in our lives, and it's a natural phenomenon that is imperative to our health. Going under anaesthesia for some kind of surgery is not the same as going to sleep naturally. Nor is being in a coma comparable to voluntary sleep because the brain activity is completely different in both cases.

Rather than being a passive activity, which sleep used to be thought of as, it's the time when our brains explode into a manic frenzy. Unknown to us, neurons at the base of the brain start signalling when we fall asleep, switching off the chemicals that keep us awake like serotonin and norepinephrine. We even know that a chemical called adenosine may build up in our blood before sleep, causing us to feel drowsy and eventually leading us to nod off.

Once we do doze off, the brain springs into action as it begins to process everything we've experienced during the day while firing up mechanisms that restore our cellular well-being. It's a very cool trick if you think about it because it all happens without us having to make any effort at all. It's like taking your car for a full service every night without having to physically drive to the mechanic.

As we lose all awareness of what's going on around us and drift into the Land of Nod, we pass through five important stages or cycles of sleep several times throughout the night.

The first four are imaginatively named stages 1, 2, 3, and 4, followed by the fifth cycle, known as REM sleep (which stands for Rapid Eye Movement, as well as being the name of a famous rock band!). As adults or children, we spend about 50 per cent of our sleep time in stage 2, about 20 per cent in REM, and the other 30 per cent going in and out of the remaining stages.

New-born infants spend a whopping 50 per cent of their sleep time in the REM phase, so there's obviously a lot going on there that contributes to their growth and development. They gradually catch up with us from three months onward, and the fewer hours they sleep, the less REM sleep they have. So, what's going on during all of these different cycles, and why does it matter when it comes to dream interpretation?

Obviously, the quality of our sleep has an impact on how much we dream, and possibly what we dream about. Sleep is the great vehicle through which our weird and wonderful dreams play out, which is why it's good to know what is happening and how to enjoy the best sleep possible. And, as 'The Bard' himself said, "To sleep… perchance to dream."[3]

- **Sleep stage 1:**

---

[3] Shakespeare, W., Hamlet, Act 3, Scene 1, Amazon Classics, 2017

You know that blissful feeling when you begin to gently doze off but aren't quite asleep yet? That's Stage 1 of the sleep cycle during which time your body begins to relax, and your mind becomes blurry. You might even experience sudden muscle contractions known as hypnic myoclonia in this early phase and get that familiar feeling of falling.

- **Sleep stage 2:**

As you enter the second sleep cycle, your eye movements stop and your brain waves slow down. These can be measured with electrodes and if you could observe them, you would see occasional bursts of waves firing off called sleep spindles.

- **Sleep stages 3 and 4:**

Now you enter deep slumber, during which slow brain waves, or delta waves, start to become active, alongside intermittent faster, smaller waves. You are sound asleep at this point and not easily woken. If you are, it's quite likely that you will feel groggy, disoriented, and, in my case, rather bad-tempered for a while. It's also during this stage of sleep that children will suffer from night terrors, sleepwalking or bed-wetting.

- **REM sleep:**

After reaching that deep sleep state, you switch over to REM: your breathing becomes shallower and speeds up here, while your eyes dart around in different directions as if watching something happening. You can tell when someone is in the REM sleep state by seeing their eyelids move about. Not only that, but heart rate increases, blood pressure rises, and men can have penile erections. It all sounds a bit orgasmic and for good reason: this is when all of those wild and wonderful dreams come alive!

As you sleep through the night, these cycles go onto a kind of loop, which takes about 90 to 110 minutes to complete from beginning to end before it starts all over again. Some modern day "Fitbit" devices can even monitor this for you and show it on a pretty graph within the phone app for you to fascinate over each morning.

The first REM moments happen around 70 to 90 minutes into your sleep, gradually getting longer in duration as the amount of time spent in the deep sleep phase decreases. By the time you have woken up in the morning, you will have spent most of your sleep time in stages 1, 2, or non-REM mode, and REM.

All very interesting, you might say, but what is the purpose of all these cycles, phases, dream and non-dream modes? What is really happening inside the brain and why does it engage in this extremely frenetic activity while our body rests?

Why do we sleep?

Just like eating and drinking, sleep is an essential bodily function, and we can't live without it. It's our body's way of recharging and allows the brain to do some serious filing at the same time.

Matthew Walker is a leading neuroscientist and sleep expert who knows a thing or two about why we need sleep. He's looked into the subject very thoroughly during his role as Professor of Neuroscience and Psychology at the University of California, Berkeley, and as Founder and Director of the Centre for Human Sleep Science.

For Walker, sleep plays a vital role in our health, and he even suggests that we need it to repair all of the damage our brain has to deal with when awake. He's talking about the build-up of beta-amyloid in our brain — a sticky, toxic amino acid that we accumulate throughout our waking day. Not wishing to raise any alarm bells, this beta-amyloid has been found to have many negative effects on our health, including the onset of Alzheimer's disease. Now, that puts the term 'a good night's sleep' into a whole new perspective!

We can divide the function of sleep into two main components: our *bodily health* and our *brain health*.

Bodily health

- Sleep is the time when our immune system gets a good overhaul, organs are repaired, and muscles are rested.
- Our T-cells, or immune cells, sprint into action during sleep, busily going around as if they were on a serious military mission. Their job is to fight off any potential pathogens and restore our bodies as best they can.
- Sleep replenishes spent resources and hormones that dictate appetite, cognitive function, and motor skills are balanced.
- For men, sleep is a testosterone regulator, while for women, it strengthens their immune hormones against breast cancer.
- According to Walker, an eight-hour sleep also helps the body to replenish those all-important cancer-fighting cells that are our shield against malignant carcinogens.[4]

---

[4] Walker, M. P., Why We Sleep, Penguin (2018)

Brain health

- Sleep is our brain booster. It's the time when we decode all of the bits of information that we picked up during the day and transfer them from short-term to long-term memories. This is essential for when we need to recall information and if we skip sleep, a lot of what should be stored in the 'archives' can get lost or misfiled.
- It also allows our brain to reboot, just like a PC, removing all of those useless cookies, or irrelevant bits and bytes that we don't need.
- If you've ever experienced a lack of sleep, you will know how difficult it feels to think straight, concentrate, recall information, and carry out even the most mundane tasks.

Your inner clock

Nature still has a great command over us, no matter how far removed from it we think modern life has become. Inside each of us is an internal body clock that regulates our sleep cycles. This is known as the circadian rhythm, and we are slaves to it, suffering dire consequences if we try to work against it.

It operates on a 24-hour cycle and is counting down to sleep from the moment you wake up in the morning. As I mentioned above, the hormone called adenosine has been identified as the compound in the brain that increases throughout the day, making you feel more and more tired as the hours pass. It's like a kind of internal sleep drive, letting you know that sleep is required at some point, and you shouldn't delay it!

Your circadian clock is also light-sensitive, meaning that when you are exposed to natural or artificial light, that message is passed through your eyes to a cluster of cells in the hypothalamus. This helps the brain to determine if it is day or night and if you are exposed to too much light when you should be sleeping, that creates a lot of confusion.

The natural process for sleep is to do so when natural light fades, i.e., at the end of the day. That's when melatonin is also released in the body —another hormone that makes you feel drowsy. By the time the sun has come up in the morning, the body reacts by releasing cortisol, which causes you to feel alert and ready to wake up.

Mess with that natural cycle, and it's easy to understand why your sleep patterns can go haywire. This leads me to talk about what else can keep us from sleeping, and there are certainly several well-known factors.

Why can't I sleep?

There are many reasons why you might find it difficult to sleep when you go to bed or wake up in the middle of the night and are unable to go back to sleep again. Tossing and turning is no fun at all, especially if you have to get up at a certain time the next day, which can add to the frustration. As we all need a decent night's sleep of around 7-8 hours, working out why we can't is vital.

Getting to sleep in the first place is different from waking up during the night for some unexplained reason, and I'll get to that in a bit. You've probably heard that certain habits can have a harmful effect on your sleep schedule, as well as the lifestyle you lead, so I'll be taking a look at those first.

Since we now know that sleep and wakefulness are influenced by different neurotransmitters firing off in the brain, anything we do that affects those functions can mess up our sleep routine. Food, alcohol, caffeine, and some medication can all upset the natural balance, causing confusion within our bodies.

Caffeine and alcohol, for example, stimulate some parts of the brain so it's not a good idea to indulge in either before bedtime. Whenever you drink something containing caffeine or alcohol before bed, you are basically telling your brain to produce 'wake-up' chemicals instead of sleep ones so avoiding that nightcap is a good idea. Heavy smokers can also suffer from nicotine withdrawal during the night, making them wake up after 3 or 4 hours of very light sleep with an urge to smoke.

If you suffer from depression, you may find it hard to sleep and be prescribed some kind of medication to help you. The problem with this is when you take antidepressants, they can suppress valuable REM sleep, so it's a bit of a catch-22 situation. You may fall asleep easier, but the quality of your sleep is not following the natural restorative cycle needed for healthy functioning.

The room temperature can also affect how well or badly you sleep. Once you are snoozing, you lose some of the ability to regulate your body temperature so if it's too cold or too warm in the room your sleep will become disturbed. When the REM cycle is disrupted, you go into a kind of freefall and everything gets out of sync, making it even harder for you to get to sleep again after waking up.

Too much light can also seriously prevent you from falling asleep easily, as your brain doesn't think it's time for bed. Even the light emitted from your mobile phone just before shuteye can throw a spanner in the works, which is why sleep experts advise against using it before you turn in for the night. The same goes for the TV or any electronic device that is stimulating your cortisol levels.

An uncomfortable bed or pillow also affects how well you sleep and buying a decent mattress is probably one of the best investments you will ever make. Aches and pains caused by mattresses or pillows that don't properly support your body can make getting to sleep and staying that way almost impossible. It might even be better to sleep on the floor if that's the case!

Developing a healthy sleep routine can be beneficial to anyone who finds it hard to get to sleep in the first place and will go some way to dealing with insomnia, although chronic insomnia may need further expert measures.

As a general rule, there are a few simple things you can do to get into sleep mode each night:

1. Make your bedroom conducive to sleep. Create a relaxing space that you associate with sleep and remove the wall TV or any other distracting gadgets. Use blackout curtains or blinds to reduce light pollution and try to maintain a room temperature of around 18.3° Celsius (65° Fahrenheit).

2. Avoid consuming too much caffeine throughout the day. Even a cup of coffee in the late afternoon can stay in your system for 3 to 5 hours, counteracting the levels of adenosine that help you to feel drowsy.

3. Reduce exposure to screens before bedtime. It's very tempting to take your mobile to bed with you and scroll through the news, notifications and your social media feed. The problem is that the blue and white light emitted from your phone screen (or laptop/tablet) plays havoc with your sleep cycle, blocking the production of melatonin. How about reading a good old-fashioned book instead before switching off the night light?

4. Wind down before going to bed. Your day may have been full of stress or anxiety and carrying all of this to bed with you will interfere with a good night's sleep. Your brain is still in active mode and the less able you are to get to sleep, the more anxious you will become, making it a vicious cycle. Relaxation exercises half an hour before you retire to bed can help, as well as yoga and meditation.

5. Eat as little as possible before turning in. There's a good reason why experts suggest not eating anything two to three hours before going to bed. Food gets your metabolism geared for action, which is the last thing you want when you need to relax. When you lie down, gastrointestinal acid follows the law of gravity and flows back up into the oesophagus, often creating burning sensations that are not going to allow you to sleep well.

Lack of sleep

I'm sure I don't need to tell you what it feels like to have slept badly, or not slept enough the night before. The obvious symptoms are a headache and yawning, as well as feeling groggy, irritable, lethargic, and tired. Even missing 1.5 hours of sleep the night before can leave you feeling less alert, impair your memory and ability to process information, affect your quality of life on any given day, and even make you more accident-prone.

These are all short-term symptoms that a good sleep will overcome, although long-term sleep deprivation can have serious adverse effects on your overall health. Some of those potential problems have been identified as high blood pressure, diabetes, heart attacks, heart failure or strokes. Chronic sleep deprivation is also a factor in obesity, depression, reduced immune system function and lower sex drive.

Your central nervous system is highly compromised when you suffer from chronic insomnia, with your body being unable to send and process information properly. Your brain starts to run on empty, trying to maintain neural pathways that help you to retain information, but without any fuel to do so effectively.

Missing out on sleep over a long time period can also seriously affect your emotional state, make you prone to mood swings, and compromise your decision-making abilities. You could even start to hallucinate or fall into a severe mental state, such as mania, impulsive behaviour, anxiety, paranoia, and suicidal thoughts. The inability to sleep at night might cause you to nod off during the day in what is termed microsleep, during which you fall asleep for a few seconds without even realising it or being able to control it. This can be extremely dangerous, especially if you are in charge of young children who need constant supervision, are behind the wheel, or operating any kind of machinery. Scary stuff, right?

Lack of sleep is really, really bad for you and it will take its toll on your body after a prolonged duration. Your immune system is weakened, making it easier to get ill and more difficult for you to recover from those illnesses. If you have sleep apnea, which is a breathing disorder, this interrupts your quality of sleep and can make any existing respiratory diseases like chronic lung illness even worse.

When your sleep is continuously broken or not sufficient, the two hormones responsible for your feelings of hunger and fullness (leptin and ghrelin) are compromised. Leptin, which tells your brain when you are full, is reduced, and ghrelin, the appetite stimulant, increases. The imbalance in the two leads to night-time snacking and gradual weight gain. Less insulin, which helps your body to reduce your blood sugar (glucose) level, might also be released. Hormone production is interrupted too, leading to less testosterone and growth hormone production, especially in children and teenagers.

And last but not least, there's a reason why we say that we need our beauty sleep. A lack of it can cause dark circles under the eyes and premature wrinkling, due to the overproduction of cortisol that breaks down collagen in the skin. Need I say more?

In 2021, Netflix streamed the dystopian movie entitled, 'Awake'. The storyline went that a mysterious catastrophe wiped out all electronics and deprived humans of the ability to sleep, causing mass mayhem. The side-effects of insomnia threatened to bring an end to the human race as we know it, with people running around doing completely erratic things. Imagine if that were the case and we were never able to dream again…now that's a frightening thought!

Chapter 2

The Subconscious

The actor Justin Theroux said, *"There's a logic to dreams that doesn't necessarily follow linear narrative…. it's your subconscious pushing you, to give you information."*

You have probably heard something similar; that our subconscious mind is talking to us while we dream in strange symbols that we need to decode.

Do you keep having that same dream of trying to run away from something but being unable to move? Or the one where you are walking around your local High Street completely naked? Well, maybe not the latter, but I'm sure you get the picture. When we have similar themed dreams over and over again, there must be something that our subconscious is telling us, if we could only work out what it was. We also have one-off dreams or nightmares that linger with us for the next few hours or even days as we try to fathom what they could possibly mean or signify. Some of them are pretty scary, too, and you may often find yourself wondering what on earth is going on in your mind!

We credit the subconscious with a lot of power, without really knowing what it is.

How would you describe it?

Where is it located, and how can you tap into it, if at all?

These are questions that have been asked over the ages and the truth is that we still don't fully grasp what the subconscious is capable of or how it works.

Plenty of people have tried to explain it to us, from neuroscientists to philosophers and psychoanalysts, so there is a general consensus that it exists, although we still haven't got a clear picture of what it does exactly.

Meet your subconscious

We've come to understand the subconscious mind as something different from the conscious mind, which is a good start. You could compare our conscious mind to a ten-item shopping list, while the subconscious mind is a vast library filled with an infinite number of books we can't remember ever reading. We can handle the shopping list pretty easily – it's only ten things – whereas we get lost easily in the library and struggle to find even one book that makes any sense.

I've read some impressive facts about the capabilities of our subconscious, such as that it's at least 1 million times more powerful at processing information than our conscious mind. They say that by the time we have reached the age of 21, we've already stored more information in the subconscious than one hundred times the contents of the entire Encyclopaedia Britannica. It's like our own personal Google, recording billions of bits of information as we experience life, which is all there for us to access if need be.

Of course, it's not as easy as typing something into a browser. We can't always find what we are looking for and our subconscious isn't always willing to give us what we need in a manner we can understand. That's what makes it so intriguing. It may work in a weird kind of way that we aren't fully clear about, but we can't live without it.

While the conscious mind can plan, reason, act, think, and do, the subconscious mind stores and retrieves data. It ensures that you respond in the way that you were programmed to do, without you having to 'think' about it first. It's also responsible for managing your digestion, heart rate, breathing, blood pressure, as well as other important bodily functions.

Is it a real thing or an idea put forward by neuroscientists who can't understand how our brain works? Why have cognitive psychologists tried to debunk psychoanalyst Sigmund Freud's theories of the subconscious, and what difference does it make to us anyway?

Sometimes, experts find themselves arguing over what name to ascribe to a particular concept or idea. While most agree on the term 'the conscious mind', the word 'subconscious' is often used interchangeably with the 'unconscious mind'. This is a bit confusing if you consider that being unconscious also means we are either asleep, under anaesthetic, have fainted, or are even brain dead.

For me, the terms 'unconscious' and 'subconscious' are very different things. When we are asleep, or 'unconscious', it's the conscious mind that is temporarily out to lunch. The subconscious mind is still working, taking note of what's going on and constantly regulating our autonomic nervous system. I prefer to call it my inner voice, but you might call it something else, like your inner self or your intuitive self. Whatever you call it, we are talking about the part of us that operates beyond our conscious mind.

It's also the place where all of your perceptions, beliefs, habits, and emotions are stored. Just ask yourself how you felt at the birth of your first child, when you received that big promotion, or how it was to fly for the first time, and your subconscious will provide you with those emotional memories.

When you focus on doing a task or thinking about what to have for lunch, you are using your conscious awareness. Anything else that you aren't focusing on or not aware of sits in your subconscious mind. This could be driving to work or brushing your teeth – things you do day in, day out, that you don't need to think about. It's the CPU of your brain, keeping things ticking over nicely and allowing you to focus on what demands your attention at this moment.

Psychologists refer to the part of consciousness we are oblivious to as the **subconscious** – all that information we aren't actively aware of at this minute but that can influence us, nonetheless. The term '**unconscious mind**' was actually coined by Freud to refer to the place where things like desires, wishes, repressed emotions, and socially unacceptable ideas are kept. He made it sound like quite a seedy place, although that might reflect the strict societal norms, he was living in at the time of carrying out his work.

Freud's views were highly influential and continue to hold the attention of many, although a lot of what he said about the workings of the mind has not stood up to stringent scientific testing. We understand a lot more about mental illness than back in his day and don't assume that anyone suffering from such maladies has some kind of psychopathological trauma or repressed psychosis. Today, we have a completely different approach to the way we treat people with emotional issues and mental disorders.

The way the mind works has always fascinated us and, historically, it was defined according to the context, time period, culture, and knowledge. For philosophers, the mind referred to our personal identity or memories. For the religious, it housed the spirit, and for the scientist, it was a machine that generated thoughts and ideas. By the 14th and 15th centuries, a generalised idea of the mind came to prevail: it includes our mental faculties, thought, volition, feeling, and memory. Later on, in the 19th and 20th centuries, with the birth of psychology, the mind-body question came under the spotlight again, with Freud and his contemporaries seeking answers to why we behave the way we do.

Today, we take a more scientific approach to the concept of the mind and want to see facts, figures, hard evidence, convincing research results, and infographics. Nevertheless, we still have a framework in our mind, so to speak, of what our conscious and subconscious are that isn't too far removed from what Freud described all those years ago.

For him, the mind could be divided into three main levels, much like an image of an iceberg. At the top is the part we can see – the conscious (about 10% of the whole mind). Just below the waterline lies the preconscious (around 50-60%) of the mind, and the remaining 30-40%, our unconscious, sits at the bottom. All three combined make up one big reality, most of which we aren't fully aware of.

If you follow this model, the top part, or the conscious mind, is like a radar, picking up bits of information that it either stores in the preconscious mind until further notice or dismisses. The preconscious could be compared to our short-term memory if you like, holding data that you might need to use throughout the day such as the name of someone you have just met, or a conversation you had with a colleague.

When you fall asleep at night, these random bits of info get sorted either into the long-term memory (or unconscious mind) or are left floating around in the miscellaneous section of your brain.

Freud's unconscious (or subconscious) mind was where all our memories and past experiences were stored. Some are forgotten on purpose, others aren't that important to us and, according to Freudian thought, it's these suppressed memories and experiences that shape our beliefs, habits, and behaviours. They are revealed to us in disguise through our dreams, and if we can analyse their content, we can discover how those unconscious thoughts and feelings are influencing our conscious lives. Freud stood by dream analysis and free association (the sharing of seemingly random thoughts) as a means to get to the bottom of our subconscious and what it was trying to tell us. That's the theory, anyway.

Where is the subconscious?

From what we know, the subconscious can be found in the brain, and not the heart, belly, or elsewhere. It's thought to be located in the subcortical regions, which are a group of diverse neural formations deep within the brain that include the hypothalamus, pituitary gland, limbic structures and the basal ganglia. They are responsible for complex functions such as memory, emotion, pleasure and hormone production. The nervous system also receives information from this region, which is passed around different areas of the brain.

The subconscious operates independently, handling information coming from different sources, as well as picking up signals that the conscious mind might not notice. A lot has been said concerning the subconscious' ability to detect subliminal messages, which is a sneaky way for advertisers to make you buy their products, such as using product placements in your favourite sitcom. While that box of cereal doesn't seem to be essential to the plot, your brain picks up on it and the next time you go to the supermarket, lo and behold – you add the same cereal box to your shopping trolley.

Some contemporary psychologists uphold the view that our conscious mind is responsible for higher mental processes and the unconscious mind simply follows along, handling subliminal information but without having much say in how we behave. A well-known study named 'Is the unconscious smart or dumb?' counteracted that view and suggested that the unconscious mind is actually pretty smart.[5] Apart from preparing simple stimulus-response actions, delivering facts, recognizing objects, and making the body move, it can also solve equations in the blink of an eye without us even being aware of it.

Your own inner life coach

If this is the case, and there's no reason to assume why not, then the subconscious is much more powerful than we think. It may be time to give it more credit rather than relegating it to some kind of dusty storeroom that we only enter when asleep. Psychoanalysts will tell you that we can tap into the subconscious through hypnosis, a kind of 'unconscious yet awake state', to get to the bottom of whatever is troubling us.

---

[5] Loftus, E F, and M R Klinger. Is the unconscious smart or dumb? *The American psychologist* vol. 47,6 (1992): 761-5. doi:10.1037//0003-066x.47.6.761

If you have ever been put under hypnosis by a professional, then you will know that it feels like going into a sleep state without actually snoring. If you haven't tried it, imagine being totally relaxed and putting all of your thoughts and sensory antenna on mute so that you can delve into your inner vaults. During hypnosis, you are processing your thoughts through a deep, focused awareness. Some people claim it is an effective way of treating pain management and weight loss, as well as alleviating anxiety, which makes it an interesting method to try out if you suffer from either.

Obviously, you can't always run to a hypnotist when you want to access your subconscious, and you don't need to. It also isn't necessary to take some kind of illegal hallucinogenic drug or seek out an ayahuasca medicine man in the Amazon rainforest. What you can do is tap into it through your dreams if you know how to, and gain access to your inner life coach. Your subconscious knows everything about you and can give you the information you need to work things out. I'll be talking more about how to do this in the following chapters.

Every experience, thought, and feeling you have ever encountered in life is stored in your subconscious, so it's a good place to start if you want to gain a greater understanding of yourself and figure out any personal issues that may be stopping you from reaching your full potential.

How can it benefit you?

The wellness market has latched on to the idea of the subconscious as a powerful tool for self-help and you can find a lot of information out there about how to solve problems, build your self-esteem, develop a positive mindset, and even grow rich! Eastern philosophy and practices are also a popular means by which you can reconnect with your inner self, or subconscious, by practising meditation and mindfulness. With meditation, you open space in your mind for whatever comes to the surface, giving you useful insights into your life. Mindfulness allows you to observe your conscious thoughts, as if a fly on the wall, helping you to get rid of negative thoughts and stress.

There's a lot to be said for understanding what our subconscious is trying to tell us, especially today when we lead such busy lives and don't allow time to simply 'be'. We are also inundated with so much external stimulation that sleep may be the only time where we can truly rest, reflect, and process everything we experience. Tapping into that valuable reserve could give us answers to problems, clear up doubts, point us in the right direction, and help us to resolve any issues that have been on our minds.

There are also some activities you can do to become more attuned to your subconscious mind while awake such as meditation, although these need a bit of practice if you aren't familiar with them. They also require a bit of faith in the process, otherwise, you won't see the results that you might expect. It's not magic… it's more to do with opening your mind up to new possibilities and we'll be exploring some of these ideas in Chapter 8.

One thing is for sure: we no longer see the subconscious mind as a dark dungeon where our unsavoury sexual appetites, destructive impulses, and repressed memories are stored, just waiting to escape and cause havoc.

Although the debate is still ongoing about how this mega machine works, we certainly have a much better understanding of it now than we did in Freud's time. The subconscious is extremely efficient, yet it serves a completely different purpose from the conscious mind, so it doesn't add anything to the conversation by trying to decide which one is smarter. Both have something to bring to the table.

Once referred to as the "shadows of the mind," our subconscious can hold some fears, attitudes, and biases that affect our everyday thinking and actions, but that doesn't mean we have to let it dictate to us. We are capable of working through our responses and looking at ways of changing them. Psychotherapists are trained to help their patients do exactly this, and to get to the bottom of their problems by bringing awareness to hidden beliefs and fears.

These 'memories' can then be critically examined and assessed for their value, with the aim of helping people to understand their deeper feelings and enable change for the better.

Remember Matthew Walker from Chapter 1? In one of his Ted talks in 2021, he mentions the usefulness of dreams.[6] For him, not only do they serve as overnight therapy but what we dream about can also be very beneficial to us.

His studies have proved that when we dream about working through a problem, we wake up having much greater clarity on how to solve it. As all of that information in our brain is washed, rinsed, and tumble-

---

6

https://www.ted.com/talks/matt_walker_the_surprising_h ealth_benefits_of_dreaming dried, there's an opportunity for new, creative ideas to emerge. The same applies if someone is going through a difficult period in their life, such as divorce, or recovering from a traumatic experience.

Dreams help us find closure or resolution and if we can tap into that sleepy subconscious level of ourselves, it can make a world of difference to our waking lives.

Let's dive into the landscape and architecture of dreams in the next chapter!

Chapter 3

What Are Dreams?

"Keep your dreams, you never know when you might need them."
– Carlos Ruiz Zafon

While you sleep, your mind creates thoughts, stories and often images that can be entertaining, disturbing, frightening, romantic or even X-rated. These thoughts are commonly referred to as dreams, played out by your subconscious mind, which I prefer to call my inner voice.

People have been dreaming since the dawn of civilization, with the earliest recorded writings of dreams dating back to 5000 years ago that were found in Mesopotamia. You may have heard of the 25,000 clay tablets containing the world's oldest form of literature. One of them is known as the Gilgamesh Dream Tablet, which narrates part of an epic saga based on dreams.

In previous centuries, it was believed that dreams were divine messages sent to us by gods to foretell the future. Some claimed that they could also be messages sent by demons to deceive the dreamer. Ancient dream theorists were known to give more importance to the dream state than to their waking lives (but perhaps this had more to do with the natural drugs they were ingesting!).

In the 1800s, scientists believed that dreams were meaningless and caused by indigestion and other physical discomforts such as extreme cold or heat. Although this belief sat well with the people of that era, things began to change in more recent centuries as dream theorists started to consider a scientific and philosophical approach to dream interpretation.

Although this is not a history book, I will be touching on the phenomenon of dream interpretation over the centuries in Chapter 4 and the role it played in all kinds of decision-making, from whether to pack an umbrella when venturing out to choosing the best location for a major battle for crown and country. The fact is that past civilizations and cultures did it, and they did it for one very good reason... they believed it, and so do I.

What kind of dreams do we have?

Our nightly slumber is punctuated by disorganised and illogical dreams that can be totally off the wall. We might be flying, walking on the moon, or sitting on a train next to Einstein himself, making for head-scratching interpretations.

We often see loved ones who have passed away and sense that they are still with us. We might travel through time like some fantastical science-fiction movie or find ourselves transported to bizarre environments where life as we know it is turned upside down. We can experience sudden shifts in the dream landscape, jumping from one surreal scenario to the next, all of which leave us wondering what on earth was going through our minds when we open our eyes.

Feelings of falling, being frozen and unable to move, are also common experiences reported to occur in dreams, and these are common sensory sensations scientists are trying to explain. Our dreams may be quite vivid and feel very real. How often have you woken up convinced that there are hundreds of banknotes stuffed under your pillow that you frantically search for, only to realise it was just a dream?

Funnily enough, we accept everything that plays out during our dreams as 'real', no matter how strange, and don't question it at all. It's only when we wake up and remember them (if at all) that we register how peculiar they were.

Approximately 95% of that dream content gets deleted from our minds by the time we've opened our eyes in the morning. I know plenty of people who claim that they don't dream at all, which strikes me as very odd, but it's more likely that they simply don't remember them. It would seem like we have very little control over the content of our dreams and how long we remember them for.

If you suffer from insomnia, which might include waking up in the middle of the night on more than one occasion, your dream recall is probably heightened, and this could reflect the stress you feel about waking up and not being able to get back to sleep. A friend of mine with chronic insomnia remembers 4 or 5 of her dreams each night because she is constantly waking up just after they occur. Her dream journal must be a crazy ride indeed!

It's also interesting to consider *who* you dream about. Do you see the same person over and over or people from your past? What about appearances from people you hardly know or haven't seen for years? One study carried out by a team at Harvard Medical School in 2008[7] about character recognition found that:

---

[7] Kahn, D., Stickgold, R., Pace-Schott, E.F. and Hobson, J.A. (2000), Dreaming and waking consciousness: a

- 40% of characters featured in dreams represented a person known to the dreamer
- 35% of characters were identified by their relationship to the dreamer, or by their social role, such as a doctor or teacher
- 16% of characters featured were not recognized
- Of those known characters, they were recognized either by their appearance, their behaviour, their face or by "just knowing"

It looks like we dream a lot about people we know, but also meet complete strangers there too, who seem to pop up without any rhyme or reason. Who do you see the most often, your family members, friends, past loves, or your postman?

I'm sure that you have had dreams about someone or something that you have seen

character recognition study. Journal of Sleep Research, 9: 317-325.

recently. This is called dream lag and it tends to reflect certain types of experiences that haven't been stored in the long-term memory yet. You might also remember things from childhood in your dreams, or witness memories of an event that happened to you long ago. Why this occurs, we don't really know but it might be worth thinking about its relevance to your life today.

A dream theme questionnaire

Did you know that men and women tend to see different themes in their dreams? It kind of makes sense, if you think about it, but now we have the facts to prove it. When 444 adults were asked to identify frequently recurring themes in their dreams, the researchers found that men reported more dreams about physical aggression than women did, although why that happens is still an unknown.[8]

---

[8] Schredl, Michael et al. Typical dreams: stability and gender differences. *The Journal of psychology* vol. 138,6 (2004): 485-94. doi:10.3200/JRLP.138.6.485-494

Here are the top 55 themes that seem to be typical over different sample populations, in line with the questionnaire carried out. How many of them can you tick off?

1. school, teachers, and studying
2. being chased
3. sexual experiences
4. falling
5. arriving late
6. a living person being dead
7. a dead person now alive
8. flying or soaring through the air
9. failing an exam
10. being frozen with fear
11. being physically attacked
12. being nude
13. eating delicious food
14. swimming
15. being locked up
16. seeing insects or spiders
17. being killed
18. losing teeth
19. being tied up, restrained, or unable to move
20. being inappropriately dressed
21. being a child again

22. trying to complete a task successfully
23. being unable to find a toilet
24. discovering a new room at home
25. having superior knowledge or mental ability
26. losing control of a vehicle
27. witnessing a fire
28. seeing wild, violent beasts
29. seeing a face very close up to you
30. seeing snakes
31. having magical powers
32. vividly sensing a presence in the room
33. finding money
34. witnessing floods or tidal waves
35. killing someone
36. seeing yourself as dead
37. being half-awake and paralyzed in bed
38. people behaving in a menacing way
39. seeing yourself in a mirror

40.	being a member of the opposite sex
41.	being smothered, unable to breathe
42.	encountering God in some form
43.	seeing a flying object crash
44.	witnessing earthquakes
45.	seeing an angel
46.	seeing part animal, part human creatures
47.	witnessing tornadoes or strong winds
48.	being at the cinema
49.	seeing extra-terrestrials
50.	travelling to another planet
51.	being an animal
52.	seeing a UFO
53.	experiencing someone having an abortion
54.	being an object

Well? Do any of the above seem familiar? If so, don't worry — you are in good company. Most of us will have experienced a few or many of the above themes in our dreams at least once and that is perfectly normal, according to the experts.

The purpose of dreams

Sleep researcher and neuroscientist J. Allan Hobson wrote about the five basic characteristics of dreams in his 1988 book, *The Dreaming Brain*[9]. He suggests that dreaming is the brain's attempt to make sense of the neural activity we experience while asleep, which is why it can often be so confusing. Dreams can be very emotional and even so intense that they force the dreamer to wake up abruptly. When this happens, it could be due to genuine fears or concerns about something unfolding in their life at this present time.

True story: A 30-year-old woman starts seeing a therapist to help her deal with the panic attacks she had been experiencing lately. In one particular session, she begins to tell her therapist about a dream she had

---

[9] Hobson, J. A., The Dreaming Brain: How the Brain Creates Both the Sense and the Nonsense of Dreams, Basic books, 1988

had the night before, in which she was bound up with rope in her car and unable to move. She had woken up feeling very distressed and that feeling stayed with her throughout the day.

After recounting the dream, she asked her therapist, "What do you think it means?" The reply she received was, "What do *you* think it means?"

The woman didn't know the answer at that point.

Did it mean anything at all?

Was her dream describing her problem and suggesting a way for her to overcome it?

What is your take on that?

Today, many dream theorists believe that they give insight into the character of a person and the conflicts that they are oblivious to in their waking life. This is something I wholeheartedly subscribe to and has been proven to me many times in the decades that I have been recording and analysing my dreams.

Others believe the content of our dreams is directly related to our activities during the period before we fall asleep, our emotions and thoughts in the hours before we turn in, or even what we have consumed right before we sleep. (Cheese often gets unfairly blamed for any particularly "out there" dreams.)

I prefer to go with the partly-proven theory that dreams are a direct result of sorting through and organizing newly gained memories, moving older memories from short-term to long-term storage areas and archiving off any memories that have not been accessed in a while – a bit like doing your daily PC clean-up (or for those old enough to remember, "defragging your disk").

I have come to believe that in the process of filing away all my day's experiences, thoughts and feelings, my brain can spot things that my awake self does not. Whilst I am asleep, my brain is in the best possible position to see things I might be doing that are not beneficial or good for me. It can detect anything that is generally going to cause my brain (or body) more work in the future. So, it makes sense to me that my brain would then try to warn me or gently persuade me, through my dreams, to make changes.

If I do not heed such messages, I end up having the same dream over and over until I work it out. As soon as I manage to do so, the dream stops, thereby backing up my belief that my brain notes that the message has been received and can go back to its nightly filing. It may of course be a complete coincidence or a whole load of coincidences, but it certainly works for me, which is why I am sharing my method in the hope that it might help you too or give you a good laugh – whichever is fine by me. Laughing is one of my favourite pastimes and is equally as good for you as a decent night's sleep.

Most vivid dreams occur at a specific point in our sleep, or REM sleep, which we talked about earlier. During this stage, our heart rate and blood pressure rise significantly, our breathing becomes irregular and rapid and, slightly worryingly, our muscles also become temporarily paralyzed! Waking someone who has reached this stage of sleep may not be easy, and you will find that they often speak incoherently or as if they are still not quite awake. They can also become disorientated for a few moments before they realise, they are awake and back in the conscious world.

That said, dreaming is considered a normal and healthy part of sleeping, but there can be some parts of dreaming that interfere with our sleep and mental health. Commonly called nightmares or night terrors, they tend to make it difficult to go back to sleep once experienced. If you suffer in this way, please note that this book is no substitute for advice from a medical or psychological professional in such circumstances.

Dreams can show us parts of our deepest selves, reveal our hidden wants and desires, our fears and weaknesses, emotions, and feelings. This can be scary stuff, particularly if the "head-in-the-sand" approach to life is your preference. They can be a window into what's wrong with our relationships, expose our deepest sexual needs and desires, reveal our insecurities, and even reinforce romantic attachments, so there's a lot to learn from them.

A new study released in April of 2022 claims there may be an evolutionary reason why our dreams are so bizarre, as they help us to learn and form generic concepts from previous experiences. Researchers at the University of Bern came up with the findings after using machine learning-inspired methodology and brain simulation for non-REM and REM sleep. Whatever we learn during wakefulness can, in effect, be used in our dream state to create realistic new concepts.[10]

---

[10] Nicolas Deperrois, Mihai A Petrovici, Walter Senn, Jakob Jordan, (2022) Learning cortical representations through perturbed and adversarial dreaming *eLife* 11:e76384.

If you see a dog with big ears while awake, for example, that is stored in your short-term memory during non-REM sleep and might cross over into REM sleep as a giant dog with even bigger ears. While non-REM dreams tend to mirror our waking experiences, REM dreams use creative licence to morph them into something similar, while reinforcing them as a concept. Perhaps this is also why we should pay even more attention to those weird dreams we have because our brain seems to be much more intelligent, innovative, and creative than we previously thought.

I have come to understand that dreaming is one of the fundamental mediums of self-awareness and growth. Life-changing personal transformation can come about when we get in tune with our dreams and choose to consciously seek out messages, signs, symbols, and hidden meanings. Not only that: the method I am going to share with you is completely free, available to everyone and non-scientific.

Why learn to interpret dreams?

Why not just ignore them, blame it on the after-dinner cheese you ate and get on with your day?

Getting to the real meaning of a particularly strange or memorable dream is liberating. And if it is a reoccurring dream you are trying to decipher, then it has the added advantage of letting you move past it and on to something else (such as unbroken sleep, for a start).

Some messages are small and seemingly insignificant. I once decoded a dream that resulted in me simply removing a food item from my diet to reduce bloating – a relief, I can tell you. Other dreams have led me towards much bigger changes in myself and my behaviour but have ultimately improved my relationships with friends, family and, more often than not, co-workers.

Through my dreams, I have learned so much about myself and others. I have made personal improvements along the way as a direct result of correctly deciphering the scenes I play out to myself in my dreams. It has allowed me to be honest with myself and accept when I am making mistakes, acting recklessly, or being insensitive to others. It is my hope that this short read will enable you to do the same.

I no longer cringe when someone wants to recount their dreams to me. I listen in fascination and typically learn something new and interesting about the dreamer each time.

But these are *my* benefits; the positives *I* have received as a result of decoding *my* dreams. Let's look at the wider potential benefits in more detail. Hopefully, some will stand out for you as something you wish to achieve.

Maintaining privacy and dignity

Dreams are ultimately gateways to the soul. For me, they can show us what state we are operating at, and if we are going in the right direction, without the need to bare our souls to anyone else and risk being judged, criticised or labelled in some way. Even with the best non-judgemental friends or therapists in the world, there are parts of ourselves we'd rather were kept hidden. Having the ability to decode your own dreams allows you to work on these things without the risk of shame or embarrassment.

Empowerment

Being able to interpret your dreams properly is an empowering process. It connects you to your emotions, intellect, intuition, instinct, analytical mind, and your inner spirit. All aspects of you come alive during dream analysis as you are given permission to think from all sorts of angles and perspectives.

A portal into the past

I don't know about you, but I cannot remember a dream beyond about 5 minutes after waking, so my dream journal is beside the bed and contains scrawls in all kinds of half-awake handwriting. I am thankful it is there because sometimes I fall back asleep and then when I awake properly, I have already forgotten the previous dream.

Even though most of us dream between 4 to 6 times per night, we forget about 50% of their content after five minutes. By the time we wake up, those earlier dreams are long gone, although we might remember the last one we had. That's why having a dream journal next to your bed is useful as you can write it down before it fades into the early morning mist.

If you wake up naturally and without an alarm clock, there's more chance that you will remember your dream or dreams. Focusing on them once you wake up will help you to remember them and give you time to write them down.

I find it useful to be able to look back at past dreams for any patterns or themes – especially if a dream feels vaguely similar or familiar in some way. I will read back through my journal and invariably find something I had forgotten about from a while back.

Shadow self-integration

I stated this would not be a scientific or psychology book, so all I need to say for now is that each one of us has an inner darkness, called the *shadow self*. It is usually associated with our sexuality and primal, raw, and instinctual needs and passions (but not always). These are the parts of ourselves we tend to want to deny, reject and repress. It may be that we believe they won't be accepted by society or are parts of ourselves that make us unlovable.

Through dream interpretation, you become more conscious and aware of your shadow self. With awareness comes self-acceptance. You also start to feel a deeper appreciation of your shadow, eventually seeing the beauty in your inner darkness, flaws, and faults.

My shadow used to be so huge some years back that it became very difficult to repress. Then I started being honest with myself and listening to what my mind was telling me through my dreams. I worked on the issues raised one by one and, over time, my shadow self-shrunk back into balance. I started to like myself again and realised I was no longer sick of the tunnel, with its tiny flickering light getting no closer in the distance, I could at least see a road ahead.

Today, I value my shadow self, I appreciate its purpose. There are of course still parts about myself I hide and would like to change, but I regularly remind myself that...

"Stars don't shine without darkness."

It's not easy to begin interpreting your dreams but once you do, you will start to see the value in it. Not too long ago, dreams were thought to be a window into our psyche, and we'll be looking at how that idea continues to influence dream analysis in the next chapter. Until then, I'll leave you with some weird and wonderful facts about dreams to reflect on.

- *12% of us dream in black and white, while the rest do so in colour*
- *The average person spends six years of their life dreaming in a normal life span*
- *Only 4 percent of our dreams are about sex (honestly…!)*
- *Most animals, including mammals, birds, reptiles and fish are also thought to dream, although we can't say for sure what about*

Chapter 4

The History of Dream Analysis

"I think that it is a good plan to bear in mind that people were in the habit of dreaming before there was such a thing as psychoanalysis." – Sigmund Freud

Since the dawn of time, humans have naturally lived in two different states – the waking one and the sleeping one.

I say 'naturally' because you can also experience altered states through the use of hallucinogenic plants or drugs, under anaesthetic or hypnosis, with brain damage, on fainting, through lack of oxygen, when having hallucinations, and so on. These aren't natural states of consciousness; some are induced, and others happen as a result of illness or other unfortunate factors.

But falling asleep and waking up are as natural as sunrise and sunset.

It's within the sleeping world that we experience dreams, which have been attributed with a whole set of different meanings throughout history.

They have been seen as everything from warnings and omens to divine messages and holy revelations. For most of the past 200 years, they were tools psychoanalysts could use to investigate our inner conscious and shed light on our mental or emotional issues. Nowadays, dreams are studied not so much in relation to what they mean (if anything), but as part of our overall brain functioning and development. I am optimistic that this will change as we move forward and that more will be done to study the messaging encoded in dream content and its provision of solutions to life's problems, as well as proving the long-lost beliefs of our ancestors.

From superstition to science

It's been a long journey from seeing dreams as powerful symbols or predictors of future events to neurological activity that acts as a kind of 'disc clean-up' every night.

The thing about dreams is that they are often very vibrant, sometimes disturbing, usually very graphic, and almost always difficult to understand. Maybe that's why they were given such importance in ancient civilizations, where people's perceptions were fuelled by superstition, insecurity, lack of scientific knowledge, and fear of the unknown. It's not difficult, if you think about it, to imagine that people living thousands of years ago relied on dreams as some kind of divine intervention from the spirit world or messages from the gods. When you believe in the supernatural, you are always on the lookout for evidence of that.

From the Epic of Gilgamesh on those Sumerian stone tablets I talked about in the last chapter to Joseph and his technicolour dream coat of the Hebrew Bible (Genesis

37:11), dreams were seen very early on as having great power. The Old Testament is full of stories about God speaking to various characters through dreams, such as Samuel, Daniel, and Balaam. In the New Testament, Joseph (the father of Jesus) receives God's messages through dreams and even Pontius Pilate's wife claimed to have seen Jesus in hers.

Funnily enough, most of the ancient history we know about dreams mainly features stories of great kings or leaders having weird visions that help to save or destroy kingdoms, prevent catastrophes, and sometimes even cause them. King Gudea of Sumeria, who lived around 2144 to 2121 BCE, built a grand temple because of a dream he had seen, while King Ashurbanipal of Assyria (668 to 627 BCE) was inspired by the goddess Ishtar who appeared in his dreams to gain an unlikely military victory. Dreams tended to feature a lot in power struggles, warfare, and as precursors for prophetic events about natural catastrophes and acts of God.

In Ancient Egypt, some priests worked as full-time dream interpreters, giving counsel to the pharaohs about how to handle state matters. These holy men (and women) had access to the mysteries of the dream world that existed between the land of the living and the afterlife. They acted as translators if you like, able to grasp the significance of what the Sphinx told the dreamer through the use of sacred rites and rituals. Dreams were so important that they were chronicled and recorded in hieroglyphs within tombs, serving as possible gateways into the realm of the gods.

There isn't much archaeological evidence about the dreams of the average man or woman on the street in those times... for obvious reasons. Only the rich and powerful had the luxury of being able to leave their mark on history or have stories written about them. But I'm sure that the slaves, servants and merchants of the day also had prophetic, ominous dreams because it was part of the cultural belief system. They may have dreamt about crops failing, illness in the family, or saw mythical monsters invading their slumber, to which they attributed some meaning that made sense in their daily lives.

Back then, dreams weren't about your inner psyche. They were messages from the grave, voices from your ancestors, warnings from the gods, and omens of things to come. They were, in fact, supernatural, magical, mystical, and meaningful.

The Greeks believed that dreams could be incubated to help cure illness, and their symbols decoded using dream interpretation or *Oneirocritica*. Anyone wanting advice or a message from the gods could go to a temple and, for a small payment, sleep in a special room set aside for dreaming. Sometimes, the actual dreaming itself was carried out by an oracle or seer, who acted as a link between the troubled pilgrim and the dream world and was able to decipher the messages from the gods.

Muslim scholars of the Middle Ages dedicated a lot of time and energy to studying dreams, seeing sleep as one of the great signs of the Creator, Allah, based on a mention in the Qur'an to that effect (Sūra: 30, verse: 23). Whole tomes were written on how to interpret dreams, which were seen as either false, true, or pathogenic, and the use of a professional dream specialist was recommended if you wanted to get to the bottom of them. Around this time, scholars like Avicenna started to talk about dreams as having emotional, mental, and moral aspects, while Ibn Shaheen recognized that dreams meant different things to different people.

The Chinese were also great believers in the power of dreams and contemplated profound questions about them, such as how we know we are dreaming or awake. There's a very famous anecdote in the Taoist sacred scriptures about the philosopher Chuang Tzu, who one night dreamed he was a butterfly. He flitted from flower to flower, enjoying the sense of freedom and was convinced that he was, indeed, a butterfly. When he woke up, he realised he had been dreaming but then asked himself: "*Was I Chuang Tzu dreaming I was a butterfly or am I now really a butterfly dreaming that I am Chuang Tzu?*"[11] Mind-bending stuff, which just goes to show that dreams have been fascinating us for centuries, as they still do today. During the 12th century in Europe, dreams came to be seen as evil, representing temptation from the devil himself. Through dreams, Satan could poison the mind and lead us into sin and wrongdoing. The battle between good and evil played out even in our dreams, as the Church tried to encourage sinners to repent and turn to God. Black magic and the dark arts were at a peak, causing suspicion and superstition to abound, with dreams being just one more aspect of private life that became part of the public domain. Witch burning, exorcisms and persecution were real threats to anyone

---

[11] The complete work of Chuang Tzu, Columbia University Press, 1968

claiming to be a healer, seer, or having access to the mysterious world of dreams.

Around the same time, something called dream visions also became popular. These were Mediaeval poems and pieces of literature said to convey some kind of spiritual truths using symbols and narratives. These dream visions used a literary technique called "frame narrative", which involves one story being told within another, often with the aid of a saintly guide or angel.

The most well-known example of this kind of work is probably George Chaucer's *Canterbury Tales*, and other books such as *The Romance of the Rose* by Guillaume de Lorris, the anonymous poem *The Pearl,* and *The Book of the City of Ladies by* Christine Pizan. Check them out if you are interested in what they had to reveal about life and death in a religious context.

In the 17th century, a relatively unknown physician named Sir Thomas Browne wrote about how to interpret dreams. An alchemist and philosopher, he was one of the first to discuss the unconscious psyche that was often revealed while dreaming and he even claimed to be a dreamweaver – able to manipulate events of his dreams at will. His ideas on the meaning of symbols in dreams would later influence Carl Jung in his work on psychoanalysis.

With the development of scientific thought in the West, dreams began to take on a less important role, relegated to being the result of things like indigestion and anxiety. When the neurologist Sigmund Freud (1856-1939) published his ground-breaking book, *The Interpretation of Dreams,* in 1899, he put them at the centre of psychoanalytic research[12]. This was his 'scientific' answer to dealing with patients suffering from neuroticism and hysteria, but it wasn't until much later that the study of dreams and sleep research was carried out under laboratory conditions.

---

[12] Freud, S., The Interpretation of Dreams: The Complete Definitive Text, Basic Books, 2010

Eugene Aserinsky and Nathaniel Kleitman were the first to be credited with discovering the characteristics of REM sleep using electroencephalogram (EEG) testing on their subjects in 1953. Dreams now became visible phenomena that we could study, monitor, and analyse. Since then, technology has allowed us to have a much deeper understanding of how the brain functions during sleep, and dream activity continues to surprise and intrigue us all.

Psychotherapy

You may already be familiar with Freud's ideas about the meaning of dreams, which are said to reveal our unconscious wishes, desires, and conflicts. He talked about someone's psyche, or soul, and said it was made up of three different parts:

- **The id**, which represents the unconscious sexual or aggressive drive of an individual that may not be acceptable to moral society.

- **The superego**, which represents the conscience and its internalisation of societal norms and morality.
- **The ego**, which is conscious and tries to coordinate the instinctual drives of the **id** with the taboos of the **superego**.

Freud saw this conflict between the id and superego as being at the heart of neurosis experienced by his patients. Through talking to them about their dreams, he created a model for interpreting them and believed that they contained both *manifested* aspects (dreams we remember) and *latent* aspects (those we don't remember) that sit in the *id* or unconscious.

These unremembered dreams were made up of experiences from the day before, sensory impressions during sleep, and the repressed desires or sexual drive of the dreamer. By analysing them, Freud claimed to be able to resolve those unwanted emotions, experiences, and impulses and help cure mental problems like hysteria. It's interesting to ponder just how many hysterical patients he met (most of them apparently women…), although the term itself includes symptoms like convulsions, paralysis, blindness, epilepsy, amnesia or unexplained pain.

In Freudian thought, dreams were unfulfilled wishes that we couldn't act on in our waking lives and they contained a lot of sexual symbolism. For example, the number three represented the penis, as did anything of a phallic shape, such as trees, umbrellas, and even swords or snakes. Women themselves appeared in the form of wood or paper and fruit represented their breasts. Female genitalia was presented in the guise of things like caves, windows, the mouth, or anything that could be entered.

Precious jewels or treasure could signify a beloved person while dreaming of sweets revealed sexual delight. Masturbation may manifest itself in sliding and fear of one's teeth falling out means fear of castration. Sexual intercourse could be symbolized through various scenes involving a range of male and female symbols.

As simple as it sounds, it takes someone highly trained in Freudian analysis to understand everything that needs to be taken into account while trying to interpret dreams based on this model – but have no fear, the process outlined in this book is far simpler and something you can do yourself with ease. Freud is often mistakenly quoted as saying, "Sometimes a cigar is just a cigar," which will be useful to bear in mind when thinking about the symbols you see in your dreams.

Although interested in the interpretation of dreams as a way to treat neurosis, Freud was adamant that it needed a trained psychoanalyst to do this — the patient couldn't do it alone. Once the therapist had explored the latent content of the dream, he could understand its meaning through the use of free association. It was a pretty subjective method: the therapist asks the patient to share their thoughts, or even list words, such as dog, apple, red, and so on.

While doing so, they may reveal repressed memories and emotions that the therapist could connect to treat their illness.

Like his mentor, psychiatrist and psychoanalyst Carl Jung (1875-1961) also believed in the existence of the unconscious but didn't see it as something instinctual, sexual or primal. Rather, dreams were a way to get to know your unconscious better and to understand your true feelings. They could serve as a guide on how to approach life and offer solutions to problems. For Jung, the *ego* was the sense of *self,* while the *counter-ego* was the side of you that you don't want to acknowledge. Remember the shadow self I mentioned in the previous chapter? This is exactly what Jung was talking about and he believed that you could unlock those messages if you knew where to start. He also maintained that you could interpret your own dreams in any way that felt right to you, which held more weight than how someone else might explain them.

Jung formulated the idea of a collective unconscious, noting that certain dream symbols were universal to everyone as they were inherited from our ancestors. These seven symbols or 'archetypes' of his were:

1. The Persona – the public mask you present to the world. When you dream, this persona, or Self, might appear as a dancer or a soldier, but you still know that this person is you in the dream.

2. The Shadow – which I mentioned above, is the part of you kept repressed that you don't want the world to see. It symbolizes weakness, fear, or anger and appears in dreams as a pursuer, murderer, or beast.

3. The Anima/Animus – both the male and female aspects of yourself, appearing in dreams as a feminine or masculine figure. These forms remind us that we need to accept both our assertive and emotional sides.

4. The Divine Child – your true, pure self, symbolising innocence, vulnerability and helplessness, as well as revealing your aspirations and full potential. This may be represented in your dreams as a baby or child.

5. The Wise Old Man/Woman – a figure who is there to guide and help you in the form of a teacher, priest, doctor, or any kind of authority figure.

6. The Great Mother – a nurturer, just like a real mother or maternal figure, giving you positive reassurance. On the other hand, an old witch might symbolise death or seduction.

7. The Trickster – a jester who will make sure you don't take yourself too seriously or misjudge a situation. The trickster takes on subtle forms and may embarrass you in public or expose your weaknesses.

These kinds of archetypal dreams are usually experienced when you are going through a particularly difficult or transitional period in your life. They can leave you with a sense of awe, making you remember them for a long time afterwards. If you keep a dream journal, you may see a pattern of the same images or personas appearing and this can give you insights into what these figures mean in your life.

A lot of other influential dream therapies followed those of Freud and Jung, including *Gestalt therapy*, which maintained that dreams are existential messages we send to ourselves that can be explored with a therapist. *Existential art therapy* also gained traction, during which the therapist acts as a witness to the patient's journey of self-discovery through art.

Today, dream analysis isn't widely recognized in psychotherapy as a way to help patients overcome their problems, although many trained psychoanalysts still maintain it has some use. What's clear is that a lot of people seem to benefit from dream analysis, especially those being treated for post-traumatic stress syndrome and chronic nightmares. In image rehearsal therapy (IRT), for example, the patient is asked to rewrite the nightmare or relay it and change the story into a positive one. They are then asked to go through the revised script several times a day. The Journal of Clinical Sleep Medicine has even recommended this kind of therapy as a best-practice standard for the treatment of night terrors, which is interesting.[13]

Whether you agree with Freud's interpretation of dreams or not, there's no doubt that he, Jung, and others, brought the purpose and value of dreams into the scientific spotlight. Their ideas made a great impact on psychotherapy for decades and both Sigmund Freud and Carl Jung are recognized as two of the most influential psychiatrists of all time. They coined terms like; the collective conscious, introversion and extroversion,

---

[13] Best Practice Guide for the Treatment of Nightmare Disorder in Adults Standards of Practice Committee, R. Nisha Aurora, M.D., et al., 2010, https://jcsm.aasm.org/doi/10.5664/jcsm.27883

the ego, the psyche, the persona, and many more, all of which we still use today.

One of the flaws of psychoanalysis is that most of the beautiful Freudian theories were based mainly on case studies of adults within a particular population and it's difficult to adopt them as a general theory. They also tend to suggest that we humans are all driven by some kind of unconscious force, leaving no room for free will or decision-making, which goes against what we believe today about having independent thought, a sense of agency, and being capable of self-development.

Despite that, psychotherapy is still recognized as a way for people to work through their problems. It's basically the act of talking about what is troubling you with a trained professional, who can steer you toward some kind of resolution. We all know what a good natter with a friend can do to take the weight off our problems and in the hands of an expert, it can be truly beneficial. The same applies when you engage in any kind of self-dialogue or journaling that allows you to lay out your troubles and consider them from various perspectives.

Delving into your dreams can be just as helpful, although the current opinion on dream interpretation is mostly seen as verging on the woo-woo side of life. It's not something taken seriously by the majority of the population, who have grown up in a culture that relies on science for the answers to everything. If it can't be tested in a lab, then it's not worthy of being taken seriously for most people. That's ironic when you consider that the more advanced medical knowledge becomes, the more researchers are discovering about the important role of the unconscious mind during sleep and dreaming.

It's often the case that public opinion takes a while to catch up with scientific breakthroughs. Cloning and artificial insemination are just two examples of this. When advances were first made in these two fields back in the 80s and 90s, it seemed like science fiction was becoming a reality, and not everyone was ready for that!

Often, what is scientifically possible is unpalatable for society as a whole, until shifts in public opinion gradually change as we get used to the idea. There's no reason to doubt that as science advances, it will shed more light on the importance of dreams in our lives. Apart from emotional processing, memory consolidation, and improving cognitive performance & creativity, dreams still have a lot of secrets to reveal to us and the researchers know this.

With most of us spending a large part of our sleep time in dreamland, it makes me wonder why so many people dismiss them as irrelevant. You have probably shared a particular dream you had with a friend, family member or colleague at least once in the past. Why did you do that? Is it because it was so bizarre that you needed to get it off your chest? Is it because you felt it needed to be analysed for a deeper meaning, or did you share it to make them laugh?

Whatever the reason, it seems that we do still see dreams as something mysterious...we just can't figure them out. At the same time, nightmares can leave us feeling so disturbed the next day that we want to talk about them as if to exorcise them from our minds. Being more curious about them could untangle some of their secrets and even help us to understand ourselves better.

If you never think about your dreams, how can you gain a greater understanding of what they might be trying to tell you? On the other hand, when you journal your dreams, you can start building up hard data to help you interpret them.

Until then, it doesn't cost anything to be more curious about your dreams. After all, if science still thinks they are worth examining, why don't you?

On a personal level, I think that the Freudian and Jungian dream theories still have a lot to offer for dream interpretation as they get us to think more about what our unconscious is trying to say. We all have unfulfilled wishes and desires, so it's worth taking the time to note any dreams you remember to glean information that might help you to achieve contentment in life. Your fears, anxieties, and worries can come forward in your dreams and thinking about them may help you to work through any dilemmas and problems you are currently facing.

You can be your own therapist, in true Jungian style. What have you got to lose?

"A dream that is not understood remains a mere occurrence; understood it becomes a living experience." — Carl Jung

Chapter 5

Dream Interpretation in Ancient Cultures Around the World

Depending on where you were brought up, you might have a different idea to me or the person next to you about dreams. That's because the way we view dreams has a lot to do with the culture we were raised in. If you've grown up in the West, you probably make a clear distinction between what you see while dreaming and what you do in your waking life. Dreams are just dreams, right? They aren't real, even though you might feel, like me, that there is some insight to be gained from them that can help you untangle personal issues.

For the most part, though, you've probably come to see dreams in relation to the cultural template that you adhere to and understand them within that specific framework. It's long been recognized that dreams are perceived collectively from this standpoint and, unless you've been exposed to a very different way of looking at them, your mindset will reflect that of the cultural norms. You might be fascinated by them, believe they have some kind of symbolic meaning or claim your unconscious mind is trying to tell you something, but that's about it.

The story is very different if you grew up in one of the many indigenous societies that still exist around the world, such as First Native Americans or Indigenous Australians. Rather than being dismissed as figments of our overactive imaginations, dreams are deemed to be extremely important sources of information for some cultures. They can reveal a lot about ourselves, the spiritual world, and even the future. They might be spaces for action or a way to communicate with departed loved ones and ancestors. In fact, some societies consider dreams to be so important that they are classed as *'dream cultures'* by anthropologists and sociologists.

In places where dreams are taken seriously, people have a rich way of talking about them and an expansive knowledge of how to observe and interpret them. I think it's useful to take a look at some of these different dream cultures and maybe expand our own understanding of what dreams can offer us, even if we grew up with western ideas of what they might mean.

One thing is for sure – the way we think about dreams is based on four things:

1. The beliefs we have about the nature of dreams
2. The way our society interprets dreams, if at all
3. The social context in which we share or don't share our dreams

4. The ways dreams are used in practice, such as in healing or therapy

Although we view dreams as something personal and subjective, in some cultures they belong to the public domain. While we separate dream life from real life, others see them as a different 'life space'. They may also be portals into a different kind of reality, sources of supernatural knowledge, or channels of communication. Religious figures such as shamans, mediums or priests might act as conduits between the dream world and the waking world, bringing messages to those around them.

In truth, there are many ways of viewing dreams in different cultures all over the world. From the Asabano people of New Guinea to Sufi disciples in Pakistan, there are still societies and communities in existence that maintain a dream culture and act in line with those beliefs.

The First Nation/Native Americans

Dreams feature very strongly in Native American cultures, seen as new realms that we can't access while awake. In fact, they are so important that children in these communities are taught from a very young age to remember their dreams, which can be used as a source of spiritual guidance and healing.

It's the *shaman*, or medicine man, who has the power to heal, teach, and connect with elders who have left the mortal world through *dream walking*. As he walks through the land of dreams, he can even pass between the present and the future, gaining greater insights on his way. He enters the dream realm during rituals known as *vision quests*, which involve altered states of consciousness induced by breathwork, rhythmic drumming, and often the use of the plant-based psychedelic called ayahuasca.

Sometimes, these vision quests involve the shaman finding a quiet spot in nature to meditate or carrying out some kind of fasting ritual. Once the quest is finished, he will look for objects that back up his vision, such as bird feathers or stones.

This kind of dream travel goes back to the beginning of Native American culture, with different tribes practising a range of rituals, including a boy's transition to manhood. In this rite of passage, the initiate asks the spirits to reveal visions to help him find purpose in life. Any symbols he sees are interpreted by the elders, who share the wisdom they receive with him.

A deeply spiritual people, many Native American tribes believe that we have three souls, each with a distinct purpose:

1. The ego soul, found in the breath
2. The body soul, giving energy or life force to the body while awake
3. The free soul, which leaves the body and travels to other realms during sleep or while in a trance-like state

They also view life itself as one big dream, with everything in it being impermanent.

The dreams we experience while sleeping are part of the shamanic world, where one can access different realms, talk to animals, and gain guidance from the spirits and ancestors. They believe that it's our souls that dream, not our bodies or minds, and that some people can learn the ability to astral travel all over the world. During those astral travels, which can be achieved while in a conscious waking state or unconscious dream state, it's possible to communicate on astral planes with other souls or entities, diagnose illnesses, and find answers to pertinent questions.

The Native Americans have a complex mythology, including several creation stories. They hold that all animals were given the gift of knowing the future at the time the world was created, and individuals can call on these guardian spirit guides to help during a dream or vision quest. The *plant people* (spirits) were also bestowed with healing properties and can visit humans while they dream and give them the power to be healers, too.

Since dreams can be good or bad, talismans known as dreamcatchers are made by many tribes to protect against nightmares and bad dreams. These handmade willow hoops woven with a net and often decorated with sacred beads or feathers may be a trendy home-decor item today, but their original use was very important to Native American cultures. They acted like a spider's web, trapping any bad dreams or visions that were then destroyed once the sun came up.

The Indigenous Australians

The indigenous peoples of Australia, often incorrectly referred to as Aboriginals, are big believers in dreams and have a complete philosophy surrounding them known as *Dreamtime* or *Dreaming.* This dreamtime represents the beginning of creation, known as *Everywhen,* and includes important geographical sites formed then by the Ancestral Spirits. For the native islanders, everything is connected—man, nature, and the land—

and they keep these memories alive through legends, stories, art and songs.

The Dreaming is actually part of indigenous Australian cosmology that helps explain the creation of the universe and it brings order to everything in life. When dreaming, they pass on what they saw as a way of preserving cultural values, traditions, and laws, as well as conveying their knowledge to the next generation. Dreams can also be relayed through the use of body paint, dancing, storytelling, as well as singing, making them part of the whole fabric of cultural traditions. These traditions go back thousands of years and are still practised in indigenous communities today all over Australia and by the Torres Strait Islanders.

Dreamtime offers an ordered sense of reality and a way to interpret the world, as well as giving an explanation of how it came into being. It also lays out codes of behaviour in relationships, social interactions, ceremonies, religious activities, and just about everything else in life.

The Dreamtime stories vary from place to place, and you'll find different versions if you travel around Australia, with specific locations linked to a particular dream event. For example, Indigenous Peoples in New South Wales believe a slightly different story from those living in Western Australia about how the sun was made. Sacred sites might be anything from rocks, streams, or indents in the ground that the islanders believe to be physical traces of the First People. The land is, therefore, an essential part of their identity and has a special significance to them.

They are also custodians of the land and pass on their ancestral lineage through songlines or Dreaming tracks, which can be extremely long. They join sacred sites that trace the path of an ancestral being and can extend across the country. The elders of each community pass on these songs by word of mouth and help to keep the land alive. The most well-known spirit ancestors are the Rainbow Serpent (one of the Dreamtime Creators) and The Seven

Sisters (relating to the star cluster of Pleiades).

Because there is no concept of linear time in Dreaming, it's a bit difficult for us to grasp the idea as westerners. But for the indigenous people, life today is very much connected to the Dreamtime and Dreaming stories of the past and is part of their rich cultural heritage. There is no word for 'time' in any of the hundreds of regional languages, so the word Dreaming is a loose translation that helps to explain their ideas better. It describes the notion of moving from one 'dream' to reality, not as moving through time or in terms of past, present and future. Dreaming is always there; it is where they live, and it is life itself!

South American Peoples

When we talk about Indigenous South American cultures, here again, we are talking about a diverse range of people spread out across a massive geographical location. Within these cultures, the idea of dreams plays a vital role. Dreams establish links between reality and the invisible worlds; they connect the dreamer with their ancestors. They might reveal things like useful hunting strategies and also serve as guides when it comes to making important decisions in the future.

In his book, *La caída del cielo* (*The Falling Sky*),[14] Brazilian shaman David Kopenawa points out the differences between the way the 'white people' and the Yanomami Amazonians view dreams. The Indigenous leader points out that while we westerners *'sleep a lot but only dream of ourselves,'* the Yanomamis find purpose and meaning for their lives while dreaming.

For many Indigenous South Americans, dreaming is a kind of journey in which the dreamer can meet their ancestors and other non-human beings such as animals, plants and spirits. In that sense, the dream isn't an interior journey in the way we might

---

[14] Kopenawa, D., The Falling Sky: Words of a Yanomami Shaman (Belknap Press 2013)

view it, but more of an outward journey towards something external, distant, or otherly.

There is no 'dreamworld', but access to many worlds when asleep, which are all part of our reality, and shamans have a large part to play in that. They can connect through dreams with spiritual guides, healing masters and other beings, giving them access to great powers and wisdom. For some native communities, dreams can have different meanings and interpretations, often bringing healing and hope, or acting as a bridge between children and their ancestors.

When children dream, they are encouraged to remember them and share them with an elder, who can interpret them and make sure the ancestral wisdom doesn't get lost. It's also important to listen to the voices of their ancestors talking to them through dreams so that a constant connection is maintained.

Dreams can be a portal to another dimension that exists beyond this world, and it's even considered acceptable to *dream-share* on waking up to discuss possible hunting or fishing trips, anticipate future events, or even make prophecies of things to come. Once again, we find the idea that dreams aren't linear, but are more like circular or multilinear paths that mix the past, present and future. These motifs can be found in the rituals and stories told within the tribes as well as in their healing practices.

The Achuar people of Ecuador are a true dream culture, still practising traditional rituals that go back for generations. They wake at 3 or 4 am every morning to drink an herbal infusion made from the wayusa plant that contains caffeine before sharing their dreams with each other. This sharing of dreams is a social responsibility as it may affect the whole community, so it's important to communicate those insights to one and all. For the Achuar, waking and dreaming are one continuous existence and by sharing their dreams, they help to reveal meaning in their world. When someone has a bad dream, they are even given the opportunity to re-dream it until it becomes a more positive one, just in the same way that we can rewrite our lives.

The Asabano of Papua New Guinea

Christian missionaries arriving in Papua New Guinea around 1855 found a very spiritual people living there and immediately began to 'convert' them. Until then, the indigenous Asabano people had their own religious traditions and customs, which eventually merged with Christianity over the years. This change in belief systems also caused a change in consciousness about waking life, but they continued to see spirits in their dreams.

The Asabano people believed it was possible to contact supernatural beings during states of altered consciousness and dreaming was part of that. The aim was to access some kind of healing, learn hunting tip-offs, and find answers to practical problems through direct contact with the spirits. This was usually done with the help of a sacred man or woman, who could communicate with their ancestors and spirits.

These healers could travel to the supernatural world at night in their dreams, liaising with sprites, witches and spirits who were interfering with the lives of humans and causing sickness or misfortune. Each person was thought to have both a little soul (responsible for selfish behaviour) that stays with the body at all times, and a big soul (responsible for generous behaviour) that journeys into dreams and death. The big soul could be likened to the positive self that is capable of contributing to society.

During the 1970s, Christian Spiritualists arrived on the scene, creating a revivalist movement that focused on women said to have been possessed by the Holy Spirit. This wasn't far off from the traditional ideas of the Asabanos, who already believed that spirits could inhabit the body. This new kind of 'spirit work' became popular, with people claiming to receive visions in their dreams from the Holy Spirit about where illnesses lay in a sick person's body. Instead of being possessed by sprites, as was the traditional Asabano view, the sufferer was now seen as being full of sin, for which they had to repent.

In all the cultures we've looked at above, there is a strong sense of the importance of dreams to the individual, the community, and their heritage. Dreams are respected, revered and useful. There's also a common theme of not distinguishing between what is real and what isn't because it often doesn't matter. Our idea of reality is very rigid compared to most indigenous peoples and the idea that dreaming is a fantasy world as opposed to real life is very prevalent in our culture.

Mysticism

Although this doesn't relate to indigenous people per se, mysticism is an ancient mindset still present in many religions today that often includes the interpretation of dreams.

The sacred texts of the Hindu Upanishads date back thousands of years and divide consciousness into waking, dreaming and deep sleep. In the Buddhist tradition, Tibetan monks still practise 'Dream Yoga', which asks the dreamer to acknowledge the dream, overcome their fears, and control its content. For Sufi Muslims, dreaming is considered to be a mental state in which the devotee connects with God, and Saint Augustine mentioned lucid dreaming as a kind of preview of the afterlife.

While the Abrahamic religions (Judaism, Christianity and Islam) view dreams as a way of communicating with God, Eastern religions (Buddhism and Hinduism) see them as a means of acquiring self-awareness, both of which are interesting perspectives.

In the Upanishads, the dreamer can follow a path toward self-realisation and awareness of the illusory nature of reality. Dreaming and sleep are more important than the waking state, which is the exact opposite of how western culture has come to deem sleep. Yogic Sleep is one way to achieve this self-realisation and is sometimes compared to lucid dreaming, when we are half-asleep and half-awake. Similarly, for the Tibetan Vajrayana Buddhist, Dream Yoga is a meditation technique used to develop self-awareness while dreaming. (I'll be talking more about lucid dreaming and meditation in Chapter 8, as well as the differences and similarities between the two.)

Sufi Muslims recognize three kinds of dreams: ordinary dreams, which are based on daily life experiences that might contain our wishes and desires, dreams that reveal fundamental truths about reality that need interpreting, and dreams that offer a clear vision of divine truths. The Sufi tradition encourages the development of 'observer faculties' during the sleep stage by fasting, staying awake throughout the night, and exercises to perfect self-remembering while in a dream. These spiritual dreams come from the soul and can guide us to our true destiny and our connection to God.

For those still living according to beliefs that have been passed down for thousands of years—beliefs that form part of their identity—there is an acceptance of the supernatural or metaphysical world. Indigenous peoples are aware that they don't know everything, so they put their trust in the collective wisdom of their ancestors. Spiritual mysticism delves into the divine connection between the believer and a higher power or the inner Self to find oneness.

In both cases, there's less resistance to instinct and more acceptance of natural energies and a connection with the world around them. Dreams are complex messages of hope, guidance and well-being that are accessed from various sources, and they are always given the attention they deserve.

That's a far cry from how we have come to understand dreams and I hope you agree that there is a lot to be gained from taking a few steps back and opening up to the possibility of dreamworlds and their benefits. You don't have to live in the Amazon rainforest, join a Buddhist monastery in the Himalayas, or move to some remote Pacific island to tap into the wisdom of dreams. It isn't necessary to change your life, convert to another faith, or stop believing in whatever has served you thus far.

All you have to do is be more open to the possibilities… you might just learn something new!

Chapter 6

Common Myths

"You would have to be half-mad to dream me up."

– The Mad Hatter in Alice in Wonderland by Lewis Carroll

With so many wild and wacky myths and fallacies about dream interpretation out there, it's no surprise that most people dismiss the idea as hogwash. It tends to fall under the umbrella of astrology, palm reading and tarot cards... a lot of fun but not to be taken too seriously. But dream interpretation is a serious pursuit if done correctly, which is why I want to dispel some of the common myths about the subject.

Hopefully, I can encourage you to approach your dreams from an entirely new angle and inspire you to consider how useful they can be.

The modern 'art' of dream interpretation has been 'a thing' since the 1970s, when a book was published by Ann Faraday called *The Dream Game*.[15] At the time, the 'hippy' culture was in full swing and anything to do with spiritual enlightenment and expanding consciousness was a popular topic. Dreams might have been a stairway to heaven or a sign of the coming age of Aquarius so dream interpretation gained momentum. Faraday was a psychologist

---

[15] Faraday, A., The Dream Game, Harper & Row, 1990

who had done a lot of experimental research before going into hypnotherapy in true Freudian/Jungian style and she managed to popularise dream therapy by appearing on various TV shows during that era.

Today, a whole range of 'professional, gifted dream analysts' are waiting for you to contact them on various websites where, for a small charge, they will untangle your web of sleep stories. If you fancy checking them out, feel free, although remember that the more questions you have, the emptier your bank account can become.

You could invest in a whole bookcase of dream dictionaries, in which every possible theme you can think of is featured in alphabetical order. The explanations are usually quite ambiguous, leaving you to decide which meaning you should go with. As we tend to approach any explanation of our dreams with a certain bias, which is largely a remnant of Freud's ideas about unconscious urges and wishes, whatever interpretations you take from dream dictionaries are entirely subjective.

Factors like how much significance you attach to dreams also reflect a bias, and you might pay more attention to bad ones than to good ones. It's also likely that you are more motivated to interpret your dreams in a way that reflects your existing beliefs about life, so approaching the subject may not reveal anything new to you.

You might think that dreams are prophetic; spelling out events to come in the future. While many people have experienced this, it's difficult to always be certain that what you saw isn't simply something intuitive you picked up on before you slept. Here again, a lot of what you think may be a prediction could have more to do with your 'expectations' or what is likely or possible. For example, you wouldn't really expect to be chased by a headless ogre or thrown out of a fast-moving train in real life just because you saw those scenarios in your dreams. But you may expect an old aunt who has been sick recently to pass away after seeing her in your dreams.

It could also be the case that believing in what you see in dreams acts as a kind of self-fulfilling prophecy: if you dream that you go for an interview for a new job and don't get the position, you may wake up thinking that it's not even worth turning up for the interview. If that's the case, you definitely won't get that job because you never showed up in the first place!

Perhaps, by debunking some of the myths about dream interpretation, you will get a clearer idea of what they CAN offer you, so let's take a look at a few of those popular misconceptions.

Common Myths

Myth 1: You need a dream dictionary

In the past, I have tried several different so-called "dream dictionaries", which encourage you to look up a certain aspect or object from your dream for a standard description of what it represents. The problem with this type of approach is that everyone's situation is unique. We all have different daily battles, perceptions, and attitudes towards things. Something as simple as a cat can be a loving and necessary companion to one person, or it can be a living nightmare for someone with an allergy to cat hair. There are also different types of cats that can be dreamt about; wild hungry lions are vastly different to cute domestic kittens. The situation that the creature appears in your dream in is also quite different for everyone: a cat sleeping on your lap will carry a hugely different message than a cat gnawing away at your right leg in a brutal attack. A generic dictionary stating that dreaming about cats means this or that makes no sense to me and would be completely misleading.

The good news is that whenever you use the method described in this book to decipher advice given to you in a dream, only you will know if it is right or wrong. No one can mark you, test you, or correct you. But believe me when I say that when it comes to getting it right, in time, you will just know. You will also naturally build your own personal "dictionary", which will be far easier to remember since all entries will relate to your own personal experiences, feelings and thoughts and will have been written by you.

One of the first entries in my own dictionary was **Butterflies/Caterpillars**. For me, they appeared multiple times in dreams over a few consecutive weeks. On one occasion, I was on a park swing going back and forth and there were butterflies on either side of the chains that held the swing, pushing and steering it.

I thought little of it at first as it wasn't a particularly unpleasant dream, just a bit stressful not being able to get off the swing. A few weeks later, I had another dream where giant prickly caterpillars were more prominent, and it felt more time pressured (I was having to suck them up a vacuum pipe from all over the ceiling of my house before it was too late!) So, I decided that there was a message there somewhere and it was worth decoding properly.

After going through the simple steps in this book, I could clearly see that the two dreams were related and that butterflies and caterpillars both represented changes for me:

- The caterpillars represented planned changes that had not yet happened
- The butterflies represented the changes after they had happened

In the first swing scenario, the changes, once made, were controlling the swing, trapping me in an uncomfortable to-and-fro state (I am not a fan of swings – they make me feel nauseous after a few minutes). My brain was giving me a glimpse into the future and warning me that these changes were not a good idea and would stress me out and make me sick but a few weeks later, I still had not heeded the message. My brain then delivered a much stronger message; the second dream…

By changing the butterflies for giant, prickly (hard to handle) caterpillars, placing them on the ceiling (an upper limit), and adding some time pressure, I was now receiving a direct instruction rather than just a warning:

"The changes you are considering (caterpillars) are consuming your headspace (ceiling), and you've reached your limit (ceiling). Since they are so big (giant) and hard to handle (prickly) don't try to deal with them. Just remove them completely from the situation (vacuum them up) and do it quickly before you make yourself ill."

At the time, I was unhappy at work and had been contemplating which of two job offers to take. Weighing up the pros and cons of each had been keeping me awake at night and stressing me out. However, once I had decoded and linked both dreams, I knew I shouldn't take either of the positions. I removed all thoughts of potential changes completely at that time, politely declined both job offers and bingo; no more caterpillars, no more butterflies, no more staying awake fretting over it and losing sleep.

Our bodies cannot maintain a level of stress for prolonged periods. Eventually, our brains become sick of giving orders to pump cortisol and/or adrenaline around our bodies to keep us functioning and try to find another way to reduce the stress. My brain simply said, "This decision is yet another stress your body doesn't need right now. Let it go."

Thankfully, a change of a completely different kind happened a few months later that was perfect for me and reduced my stress levels even further.

Incidentally, I have just done a quick Google search for "what does a caterpillar mean in a dream?" and here is the first generic dream dictionary entry that came up....

> "Dreams of caterpillars can mean there is something missing from your life... Alternatively,

it can signify you are
right on track."

You're either right on track, or something's
missing? Really? Need I go on?
Steer clear of dream dictionaries. Build
your own.

Myth 2: This will only work for visual dreamers

I am one of the estimated 2-5% of the
population who has no "mind's eye" or, to
use a label created just a few years ago in
2015, I am an *aphant*.

Aphantasia[16] is characterized by the
inability to visualize mental imagery
voluntarily. In other words, your mind
cannot create visualizations or imagery at
will. You are mind blind. So, when I close
my eyes, there is only blackness. If you say
to me, "Imagine you are walking down a
beach," I can do that no problem, but I do

---

[16] There are a few different viewpoints on the concept and reality of
non-visual dreams and specifically "aphantasia". This book does not
aim to comment on the argument either way. However, I have been
taking part in research studies for the last 2 years in order to help
clarify the situation.

not *see* the beach; I will smell the sea air, feel the wind on my face, hear the sounds of the crashing waves and feel the sand between my toes, but there will be no visual aspect. It's the main reason, or my excuse anyway, why I rarely 'get' jokes that are told to me that have a visual aspect to them. My usual response is to laugh along and then whisper to someone closest to me, "I don't get it. What's funny about that?"

Visual imagery is typically considered a massive part of dreaming and dream interpretation, and some say it's integral, even essential, but I disagree. We already know that you can still have dreams, whether you have aphantasia or not. Incidentally, the word comes from the original Greek word *imagination (phantasia),* and the prefix *a-* that means *"without".* Despite that, we aphants can be very imaginative but will go about the creative process differently.

The process I share with you in this book works perfectly well for me and I believe will do for you too[17].

Myth 3: I need a therapist

You might think you need to be a psychologist or attend hours of therapy in order to understand your inner voice, but that is not necessarily true, and here's why.

During talking therapy, a trained therapist's role is to respectfully listen to you and help you find your own answers to problems, without judging you.

They provide you with time to talk, scream, shout, think, cry or just breathe. This gives you an opportunity to look at your situation from a different viewpoint. A therapist might ask you about how the dream made you feel and get you to reflect on what sensations it aroused in you.

---

[17] I am lucky – there are those who also have no ability in their mind to recall the other senses either, such as sound, smell, taste etc. If this is you, please do get in touch, I would love to hear from you.

Any answers or actions you come away with will have been decided by you, not your therapist, which is exactly what this process of dream interpretation is all about. It gives you the power and control to make progress yourself; to become your own therapist.

Although a therapist might steer the conversation in a certain direction, you are the best expert to analyse your dreams.

Myth 4: I need a psychic dream reader

A lot of people claim to have psychic abilities and that they can interpret your dreams by connecting with spirits, guardian angels, or guides from the astral plane. If this is your thing, feel free to check out some of the websites available. You can have a video call or live online chat with Tara – a 6th generation psychic specialising in romance — or with Oracle, who can predict your future by decoding your dreams. You'll also find that they have mobile apps available on Google Play or the App Store (with karma credits the more you spend).

Although many people might resort to this kind of psychic dream analysis, you really don't need to. You are capable of interpreting your own dreams and all it takes is some techniques (that I will be going over in the next chapter) and practice.

When someone claims to bring you insight into very personal aspects of your life, it just doesn't work if they are using universal interpretations that you can find in any dream dictionary. What you will get is homogenised metaphors that may or may not apply to you, which you can either accept or not. Even trained psychotherapists are usually hesitant to apply general interpretation theories to their patients, knowing full well that there is little data to back up their opinions. What they do know, though, is that the answer lies within you!

Potential Dangers

Fortunately, there aren't many dangers to be faced when interpreting your dreams. The main risk is becoming too attached or attracted to the wonder and brilliance dream decoding can bring you.

The only potential danger is the *way* in which you interpret your dreams.

The step-by-step process described in this book will help to guide you but ultimately, the key is to use your common sense.

- Use *all* your faculties; combine logic and reason with intuition and instinct
- Use thinking and feeling
- Do not rely too much on your left brain or your right
- Aim for a balanced and integrated approach

With all the introductions and warnings done, let's get started on this simple 5-step process.

Chapter 7

The Process of Dream Interpretation

"A dream uninterpreted is like a letter unopened."

— Ancient Proverb

The Process

I'm not going to fill this section with regurgitated scientific theories from Jung or Freud. What I am going to do is describe an adapted formal process that one (or maybe both?) of these neuro-nerds suggested in a long-forgotten magazine article I read many decades ago. This is how I first got started on the idea that my dreams might actually mean something.

Initially, this process seems laborious, time-consuming, and boringly academic, but bear with it, as it gets much quicker the more you do it – to the point where eventually you can…

"play the game without needing to revisit the rules."

Eventually, and with practice, you will be able to decode a dream without writing it down at all.

You will enjoy it and be eager to remember and decode the next dream. So, let's get started.

You will need:

- Notebook and pen/pencil

- Possibly a voice recorder app on your phone or maybe a Dictaphone if you have one, but neither are essential. A pen and paper will do just fine.

- A selection of highlighters in different colours

- A seriously open mind

- A normal dictionary or thesaurus is also extremely handy but not essential

Step 1 – Recording Your Dream

Which method should you use?

Audio recording

Voice recording is useful if you don't want to wake up fully and disturb your sleep too much (or that of your partner). Also useful if you are not a great writer or typist.

The idea here is that as soon as you wake and realise you remember your dream, you can grab the recorder and start talking. Following the guidelines below for what exactly you need to record, you can then drift back to sleep without too much disturbance.

I only seem to wake from dreams and remember them when it's morning. But if dreams woke me often during the night, then I might consider a voice recorder, simply because it doesn't take as long as writing and you can record so much more detail. Often, I have found that the answer is in the details.

The downside to audio recording is that you need to convert the sound to text before you can move on to step 2. That said, there are plenty of free voice recognition apps that will turn your voice into lines of typed text almost instantly.

Pen and paper

I have a nice notebook reserved specifically for dreams. It's not lined because, quite often, I scribble layouts or sketch scenes to help me remember. Occasionally, I remember symbols on things that have appeared in my dreams and so I draw them in as well.

The writing does take a while and sometimes I jot things down too quickly for fear of forgetting them and then end up with everything in the wrong order, and pages of crossings out and arrows correcting the timeline. But no matter – it doesn't have to be a literary masterpiece – just as long as I can make sense of it later. Write down key words, figures, places, symbols, or events, all of which will help to jog your memory about what you dreamt when you look over your notes.

Pen and paper are also tricky if you don't sleep alone as you usually need to put a light on to write, which can be disruptive to partners.

Despite the downsides, the pen and paper is my preferred method, simply because I can look back through it and remind myself of the dreams, the subsequent messages and lessons I have learnt.

What should you record?

As mentioned above, I find that key messages are often in the tiniest of details.

Going back to the caterpillar example, I have learnt to notice small details about the caterpillars themselves, which gives me clues as to which specific change the message is about. I now make note of all kinds of details; **texture** (prickly, hairy, smooth), **colour**, style of **movement,** and their **position** in the scene. The caterpillars being on the ceiling was significant (they were out of my reach, and I had "had it up to here with them"). If they had been on the walls, it might have been a different story… maybe telling me to stop banging my head against a brick wall and find another way forward, or maybe that the planned changes they represented would have me "climbing the walls"?

So here is a list of prompts (fitting a handy acronym "DREAM") that will help you to record all details from your dream. If you can't recall some of these things, don't fret – it typically means there's no important information to be gained there.

D = Details
- Any patterns? (maybe carpets, wallpapers, textures underfoot, etc.)

- Colours (include the shade and the detail…. vivid, muted, see-through, metallic, etc.)
- Position (in, under, atop, upside down…)
- Style or direction of movement (up, down, straight, crab-like, locomotion…)

R = Representatives
- Who is in the dream with you?
- How many of them?

E = Environment
- What's the weather like?
- Temperature?
- Light source (moonlight, artificial light, sunlight, etc.)
- Is it noisy or quiet? What can you hear?
- Any significant smells?
- Overriding colours?

A = Actions
- What is going on?
- What are people/animals/objects doing?

- Are they doing it overly well or overly badly?
- Are they injured or struggling?
- Is anything abnormal about the way they are performing actions?

M = Moment in Time
- Is it day or night?
- Dusk or dawn?
- What season is it?
- Is it constant throughout the dream or does it change at some point?
- If so, when does it change?

If you find it difficult or too time-consuming to describe, I find sketching pictures helps that I can then annotate. Remember, it's only for you, no one else will see it, so if it looks like a 4-year-old could do a better job, it really doesn't matter. The important thing is that all the details are recorded.

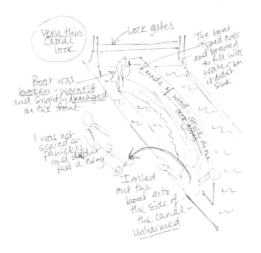

Step 2 – Mark Up Your Transcript

Take out your notebook and your coloured pens and without actually reading the transcript, just looking at the words, scan through and mark up the following:

The tangibles

The actions

The adjectives

The emotions

The Tangibles

Highlight anything that is a real object (or noun) in one colour.

- the people

- the animals, plants and trees
- the objects
- etc.

Adjectives

Next, choose a different colour and highlight all the adjectives; the words you have used to describe everything.
- rough
- high
- clean
- jealous
- happy
- yellow
- etc.

Actions

Then highlight all the words relating to actions.
- running
- wriggling
- dropped
- looking
- flew
- etc.

Emotions

After that, circle any feelings. I circle here because I have found that some may already be highlighted as adjectives (jealous, happy, tired, etc.)

"I am running, but slowly, as if hindered by something. my legs are powerless"

Spotting Patterns

At this stage, you may already start to see some kind of pattern or theme running through the dream.

It's quite possible that without even reaching step 3, you will have worked out what the dream is about simply by reading through just the highlighted words.

Nevertheless, it's important to make sure you don't jump to the wrong conclusions or see something that isn't there.

There are a couple of points to note here:

- Firstly, your subconscious will never lie to you
- Secondly, you are the expert so trust your own inner voice/guide

Step 3 – Analysis: The Tangibles

First and foremost, resist the urge to think about the dream as a whole. Look at your transcript and take each highlighted word in turn starting with the tangibles.

What does it mean to me?
What does it represent?
Have I had any memorable experiences with it?

The answers will vary greatly for everyone. Take a fence, for example. A fence can be a boundary, protection, or obstacle. But to a showjumper, it might be a goal or a challenge, and to a thief, it will likely be something wildly different indeed!

I would like to share some real examples from my experiences that may help you to see how this works.

The Bowling Ball

Every time I have ever been bowling, I have injured myself getting my fingers stuck in the holes and not being able to let go of the ball. As a result, bowling is not one of my favourite sports to take part in, although admittedly hilarious for the spectators.

When I analysed a particular dream of mine and saw the highlighted words "bowling ball" with the adjectives "heavy" and "purple", I knew it was related to either deep pain or painful bruising.

The ball had been appearing in all kinds of places throughout a number of dreams: as a photograph pinned to a fridge, in a box in the loft labelled "car boot sale". It clearly represented something I needed to explore and potentially get rid of.

Thanks to this process, that ball doesn't pop up so much anymore, but if it did, I would know that it likely represents pain or embarrassment.

Remember your subconscious is building the same dictionary as you are in your notebook.

I Can't Make Jam

Another time, there was a small detail added to the very end of a dream, almost as a parting insult, which played out as my own voice urgently reminding me that, "I can't make jam."

A small detail, but it didn't fit in with the rest of the dream and so seemed out of place and therefore significant... i.e., worth decoding.

Since I don't eat jam, this one took a while as I also couldn't think of any memories with jam in either. But by jotting down alternative names for jam, I soon realised that the term I was looking for was "preserves".

Turns out, the dream was telling me I had no self-preservation tools in place. I had left myself wide open for abuse on a particular issue. Suddenly, this passing comment now made perfect sense as part of the rest of the dream. My brain was giving me yet another warning, as well as some guidance about what I needed to do.

So don't discount anything, however weird, wacky, or out of place it might seem at first.

People and Animals

Personality traits are usually represented by other people in my dreams rather than animals or inanimate objects. I rarely feature in my own dreams to represent one of my own characteristics.

If I were to hazard a guess as to why this is, I would say that it's likely I wouldn't recognise characteristics in myself. But if another person were substituted who was well known for a particular trait, then it would be more obvious to me and, therefore, I would be able to decode the message much more quickly and accurately.

Our subconscious brains are very clever like this – it becomes like playing a nightly game of charades with yourself.

Perhaps you dreamt about someone in the accounts department at work whom you hardly know but that you see as someone who never makes a mistake – a perfectionist who dots all the i's and crosses all the t's. The dream won't necessarily mean anything sinister about the accounts person themselves or your relationship to them, but that they simply represent "attention to detail".

Or let's say you dream about your neighbour's cat that is driving you nuts by using your newly dug flower bed as a toilet. The cat itself might simply represent "irritation".

My sense of humour is usually represented by someone I find very funny. So, if I were to have a dream with Al Murray in it (a favourite British comedian of mine), it is likely to mean that there's some message about my sense of humour hidden in there.

To work out what a specific person represents, write down all the traits, attributes, characteristics etc. that spring to mind. As you progress through the puzzle, it will become clear which trait the dream is referring to. But it should be noted that, for me at least, it's usually the first one I write down (because it's the first word that pops into my head when I think about them).

Step 4 – Analysis: The Actions

Now consider the **action words** that you have highlighted. Do you perform these actions yourself? How often? Are they familiar? How do you feel about them? Are you good at them? Could you do better? Could they be causing you pain or discomfort?

Let's go back to my comedic idol, Mr Murray, and imagine he is deep in the jungle aggressively hacking down trees with a machete, I might deduce that my sense of humour could be considered quite destructive and not funny to some. I would need to address it before more people got hurt and the damage was irreversible.

So, what can seem like a very weird scene at first, often turns out to be a useful message giving me something to think about.
Don't dismiss anything – the weird and wacky are usually the dreams with the easiest messages to decode.

Step 5 – Analysing the Adjectives

Finally, look at the **associated adjectives** you have recorded with each action, for example:

- "He was running in a <u>dead straight</u> line"

- "I was running, but <u>slowly</u>, as if hindered by something, my legs were <u>powerless</u>"
- "She was swimming <u>underwater</u>, <u>peacefully</u> and <u>calmly</u>"

These will give you huge clues to add to your overall understanding of the dream.

In general, asking yourself questions about the images that crop up in your dreams can be a good way to get you thinking about their significance.

You can ask things like:

- How did I feel?
- What does the setting mean to me?
- What does this image mean to me?
- What does this action mean to me?
- When was the last time that I encountered this

place/person/scenario/fe
eling in real life?

In a way, our dreams are a reflection of our lives and of the person we are. They are like looking into a mirror, revealing details we don't often take notice of, or making us turn our attention to one particular thing. In that sense, they are an extremely useful tool for developing more self-awareness. By following the steps above, you can tap into your strengths and weaknesses, as well as gain insights into overcoming problems that affect you on a daily basis.

It's definitely an illuminating experience once you get used to it!

Chapter 8

Dream Control

"Lucid dreams help you to progress on the path to self-mastery."
– Stephen LaBerge

You can buy some smart gadgets online that claim to help you control your dreams. Simply by wearing these high-tech headsets or masks each night before you go to sleep, the manufacturers guarantee that you will be able to "...*enter a world of limitless potential.*"[18] From unlocking the power of your brilliant mind and gaining unique creative insights to even perfecting your tennis stroke, these gadgets claim to do it all by enhancing gamma activity in the brain. The technology was first developed back in the 1990s, when scientists noticed

---

[18] https://www.luciddreamer.com

that if a light was shone on a subject's face during REM sleep, they reported having more lucid dreams.

The thing is our ancestors had already mastered lucid dreaming and were even known to collectively dream and wake up to discuss any shared messages they received. They didn't have gadgets emitting transcranial alternating current simulations, or tACS, as the above headsets are known!

Unfortunately, we seem to have moved away from our natural abilities in the West as the Industrial Revolution gradually began filling our lives with machines that could do everything for us. The more dependent we became on them, the less in tune we were with our own natural resources and our deep connection with the earth. Over the decades, we've become very accustomed to a lifestyle in which instant gratification and virtual reality have replaced being outdoors and in touch with our instincts. The present generation has grown up thinking that there is a high-tech gadget for everything (there almost is…) and don't feel the need to go outside at all!

Mother Nature gave us everything we could ever need to live full, rich, satisfying lives, without the necessity to manipulate our brains with electrical noise. There are natural energy waves in the air that we can tune into but, unfortunately, most people have lost the inclination or skill to do that over time. Once we stopped tapping into our inner energy, we began seeking external stimuli, neglecting all of the potential we have within us. Instead of turning to yet more new technology to 'experience' life, we could be nurturing our innate ability to live in alignment with nature and all it has to offer us.

We already have the capacity to control our dreams and our ancestors were doing it long ago. Dreams were mediums by which they could connect with spirits and deities, as well as enter a different world — one as real as the waking world. They were much more attuned to the potential of the subconscious than we are now and relied on their senses in a way we have almost forgotten about.

Having said that, there are many people today who practise the art of dream control, which usually takes place during lucid dreaming. I have heard of cases where people can plan a lucid dream, step in and out of it, wake up and then go on to continue the same dream, manifest specific people or places in it, and even continue the same dream the next night!

But what, you may be asking, is lucid dreaming? How do you do it and, more importantly, what can it offer you?

What is lucid dreaming?

You might be surprised to hear that around 55% of people have experienced lucid dreaming at least once in their lives. It's the occurrence of being conscious during a dream, which normally happens in the REM stage of sleep, in which you can guide the narrative to a certain extent.

This kind of 'awareness' of what you will dream about has to do with metacognition, or awareness of your thought processes. Both functions (lucid dreaming and metacognition) share similar neural systems and those people who can monitor their thoughts effectively may be more likely to experience lucid dreams.

Researchers aren't exactly sure how or why lucid dreams happen, but they do know that there are some differences in the brains of those who can and those who can't. People who experience lucid dreams often appear to have a slightly larger prefrontal cortex – that's the part of the brain responsible for executive functions like decision-making and memory recall. Could this mean that the more of the self-reflective type you are, the more likely you are to have lucid dreams? The jury is still out on the findings, but studies are ongoing about the mysterious relationship between the brain and our dreams.

One theory on lucid dreaming is that it takes place when you are half asleep- half awake, otherwise known as the *hypnagogic* stage of sleep. It's that transitional phase from consciousness and wakefulness onto the sleep phase. During this transition, you might experience involuntary and imagined experiences, known as hypnagogic illusions. These can come in any shape or form and might include sights, sounds, feelings, and movement.

If you recall having this kind of experience, you will know that it's often the time when you feel you are falling, and you jerk back awake suddenly. You might also suffer from sleep paralysis during this phase, which can be quite scary. You may lose all muscle function as you fall asleep or just on waking up, unable to move or speak. People often comment that they feel weighed down by something heavy, that someone or something ominous is in the room and they might start to sweat, feeling panicky and fearful. It's a very common phenomenon and not something you should worry about.

Had a brain wave?

If you open the bonnet on your brain, you'll find that it's full of neurons constantly sending bursts of electrical activity to one another. We can measure this activity in waves using an electroencephalogram (EEG) and most research on brain function will include this clever contraption. It measures five different kinds of brain waves, ranging from the slowest to the fastest:

1. alpha waves
2. beta waves
3. theta waves
4. delta waves
5. gamma waves

While awake, your brain produces alpha and beta waves, with beta waves being predominant. As you begin to feel sleepy, alpha waves take over. When you doze off, those alpha waves start to drop off too and theta waves begin to resonate more. This is when hypnagogia happens... in that in-between stage of wakefulness and sleep. You are on the threshold of entering the dream world and might experience anything from hallucinations and body jerks to sleep paralysis and lucid dreaming.

Once you are fast asleep, delta waves kick in to offer that restorative rest you need. By the time you go into the REM stage, both beta and gamma waves occur spontaneously, which is interesting as they also appear in our waking state when we are concentrating intensely.

It's thought that gamma waves may trigger lucid dreaming exactly because of this connection with consciousness and memory during the awake state. They are the fastest brain wave of the five visible on brain scans, recognizable by their tight, consistent pattern on the EEG. Seen as a spare brain activity until fairly recently, researchers are now beginning to get a better understanding of the importance of gamma waves.

When they are triggered during meditation, which has been closely studied through the use of neuroimaging, massive gamma wave spikes tell us a lot about their benefits. Some exciting evidence comes from the University of Wisconsin-Madison, where dozens of experienced Tibetan monks took part in experiments to see what went on in their brains during meditation.[19] These are monks who state that they live in a heightened state of present-moment awareness; one in which their senses are open to an expanded consciousness and the experience of affinity with the universe.

The results showed that something happened to the gamma waves in the brain while in deep concentration. They synchronised at an extremely high level – one usually associated with robust brain function and concentration. During this process, the amygdala — our emotions sensor – was calmer and less reactive to stressful or negative thoughts. Not only

---

[19] https://news.wisc.edu/meditation-produces-positive-changes-in-the-brain/

that: compassionate meditation, in which the participant focuses on positive, loving thoughts about the world, revealed an increase in altruistic behaviour when done consistently for a few weeks.

This is definitely an interesting development, although someone who practises meditation regularly might say, "...told you so." (More on meditation below...)

A lot of famous artists, writers, inventors, and scientists have expressed how lucid dreaming helped them to be more creative or find solutions to problems. The writer Charles Dickens used a lot of the images he saw while in a hypnagogic state or when experiencing lucid dreaming in his famous books. He was a great believer in tapping into the creative potential while in these states, and even described how that felt in a paragraph in Oliver Twist, one of his best-loved novels:

"There is a drowsy state, between sleeping and waking, when you dream more in five

*minutes with your eyes half-open, and
yourself half conscious of everything that is
passing around you than you would in five
nights with your eyes fast closed, and your
senses wrapt in perfect
unconsciousness.*"[20]

Does this sound familiar to you?

When drifting off into a sweet slumber, you
might also experience visual hallucinations
of colours, geometric patterns, or images of
people or animals. You could hear sounds,
voices, music, or your name being called.
People often feel a sense of
weightlessness, flying, or falling, or get
intrusive images going around on a loop,
known as the Tetris effect.

The question is: can you induce this
hypnagogic or lucid dreaming state to tap
into your creativity, or even to astral travel?
Many of history's great minds thought so,
with Salvador Dali, Edgar Allen Poe,

---

[20] Dickens, C. 1838 in Oliver Twist, (p. 134–135)

Thomas Edison and Franz Kafka being only some of them.

What does lucid dreaming feel like?

In 2017, the academics Julian Mutz and Amir-Homayoun Javadi wrote that lucid dreaming is, "...*a hybrid state of consciousness with features of both waking and dreaming.*"[21]

It's not something that everyone might experience or be aware that they are experiencing, but it's a skill you can learn through different practices. You can develop your own capability to process autosuggestions, use external stimuli, metacognitive training (such as mindfulness) and by focusing on your state of consciousness.

At first, you might not be able to control or direct your dreams, but you can start by

---

[21] Julian Mutz, Amir-Homayoun Javadi, Exploring the neural correlates of dream phenomenology and altered states of consciousness during sleep, *Neuroscience of Consciousness*, Volume 2017, Issue 1, 2017

tuning into that feeling of being in a sleep-wake mode. Your dreams may seem fuzzy and not too clear, or they could feel very real, depending on how good you are at having them. Perfecting the art of lucid dreaming sounds like a tempting pursuit, especially if you want to use it as some kind of wish fulfilment such as meeting your 'dream guy' (excuse the pun) or flying to Cancun for a beach holiday. There's no harm in that, although it doesn't always work that way. It can take a lot of practice.

I know of someone who has been honing her lucid dreaming skills in the early sleep stages for years, which she uses to, "...*fly off and simply experience a sense of freedom and lightness*," as she puts it. Having said that, she also told me that she doesn't always manage it, especially if her mind is full of the day's events and she isn't totally relaxed.

You can raise your chances of dreaming lucidly by priming your mind before you go to bed at night. Think of what it is you want to see and go over your desired scenario as you lie there. Some other techniques that experts say can work are:

1. **Optimising your bedroom for sleeping.** Set the bedroom temperature to a comfortable 65 degrees Fahrenheit (18.3 degrees Celsius), keep the room dark and use blackout curtains or sleeping masks to help reduce light levels.

2. **Assessing your reality.** You can do this by doing 'reality testing' throughout the day. Pinch yourself every now and then and ask, "Am I dreaming?" I know it sounds weird, but with enough practice, you might be able to do the same test while dreaming.

3. **Wake-back-to-bed (WBTB).** To do this, you need to wake up after 5 hours of sleep and get up for a short while before going back to bed and trying to get into REM sleep.

4. **Mnemonic induction of lucid dreams (MILD).** For this technique, wake up after 5 hours and tell

yourself you are going to remember the next dream you have. This prompts the part of your memory responsible for remembering future plans and, hopefully, will take you to lucid dreaming.

5. **Keeping a dream diary.** Keeping a log of your dreams might aid lucid dreaming because you are more focused on them. You can combine this with the other methods to improve your chances.

6. **Using devices.** You might wish to try one of those devices and eye masks that claim to bring on a lucid state but, as I said above, you are perfectly capable of doing this naturally with patience and practice.

7. **Creating a dreamscape.** Although I am mind-blind, in that I can't visualise mental imagery, some people can. If you are good at visualisation, create a picture in your mind's eye as you lay in bed with your eyes closed. Start adding details to it… scenery, people, sounds, smells, etc. As the

scene builds up, put yourself in the middle of it and explore your surroundings. Move around and immerse yourself in the experience, enjoying this alternate reality you have created.

Many aspects of lucid dreaming still remain a mystery from a scientific viewpoint, although those who practise it don't find anything strange about it at all, including me! What they do say is that they feel less anxiety in their waking life and a greater sense of empowerment. If you can shape your dreams, you have control of your story, which could be useful if you suffer from frequent nightmares or night terrors. If you have phobias, confronting your fears in a lucid dream may help you to overcome them. There is also some evidence to support the idea that if you practise strumming your favourite guitar riff or your swerve shot shooting skills during your dream, this can improve your motor skills and your performance in the waking state.

Many people have found inspiration for their creative output through lucid dreaming, and plenty of artists have showcased those visions in their work. Salvador Dali is a well-known example and he stated in his book, 50 Secrets of Magic Craftsmanship, '...*the one most appropriate to the exercise of the art of painting...is the slumber which I call "the slumber with a key ... you must resolve the problem of sleeping without sleeping, which is the essence of the dialectics of the dream..."*[22]

Is lucid dreaming dangerous?

I've seen this question asked a lot, with many variations on replies to it. It seems that there is still a lot of superstition surrounding this kind of dream activity, which must go back a long way. It reminds me of those ancient Greeks, who used to think that when you dreamt, your soul left

---

[22] Dali, S., 50 Secrets of Magic Craftsmanship (Dover Fine Art, History of Art), 1992

your body, and could be lost to all eternity if you woke up in the middle of one.

Despite the urban myths you might have heard about sleep paralysis, lucid nightmares, and even falling into a coma or death, there is absolutely nothing to fear with lucid dreaming. It is completely safe, and you are not in any danger. After all, you are in control, so there's no risk of anything bad happening to you.

The worst that can happen is you might find it difficult to get to sleep or begin to have disruptive sleep due to the higher levels of brain activity. Here again, many people have frequent, vivid lucid dreams without even trying and suffer no after-effects in their sleep schedule, so that's something to consider.

Meditation

You might be wondering what the connection is between meditation and dream control. If you don't have any experience with meditation, you'll get some idea of what it involves below. If you have dabbled in the practice or are a seasoned meditator, you'll know that it's not as easy as it looks to get into a deeply tranquil state because your mind is constantly wandering around looking for something to do. It can take years and years of practice to achieve the ability to meditate in a meaningful way, something that Zen Buddhists know only too well.

Although meditation originated in India thousands of years ago, it's now become part of our mainstream culture and is done all over the world. There are many different 'types' of meditation but I think they can be broadly separated into two main activities: *concentrative meditation* and *mindfulness meditation.*

Concentrative meditation involves focusing your attention on one specific thing while tuning out whatever else is going on around you. The point is to truly experience the object of your focus, be that your breath, a specific word, or a mantra, as a way of reaching a higher state of being.

Mindfulness meditation includes mindfulness-based stress reduction (MBSR) and mindfulness-based cognitive therapy (MBCT). That might sound a bit intimidating, but in a nutshell, it simply means being in the present moment and making yourself more aware and accepting of any thoughts that come to mind.

As I mentioned earlier on in this Chapter, we now know that gamma waves actually increase and synchronise during meditation. Since these waves modulate perception and consciousness, it has become apparent that you can experience an increased frequency of lucid dreaming and, in effect, have more control over your dreams.

Meditation is a way to create a calm and reflective state of mind – an opportunity to be more attuned to your inward state and to reflect on that experience. When you get the hang of it, you can achieve dissociation from your physical body and awareness of the outside world, which then enhances your ability to dream lucidly. We know that meditation has a lot of other benefits, too, improving metabolism, blood pressure and brain activation, as well as bringing stress and pain relief, so it's not just about sitting cross-legged and staring at your navel.

It's also a means to achieve a restful, silent, and heightened state of alertness through concentration. You don't need to be religious to meditate and although it's a practice deeply rooted in spirituality, that doesn't mean you have to identify with any particular belief system or school of thought. This makes it accessible to everyone and as it's a completely subjective experience, you don't have to follow any rule books, carry out any kind of ritual, or reach any targets. You can simply go with the flow.

I don't want to undermine the skills it requires to become a master of meditation. Some people devote their whole lives to that and it's not like going to the gym once a week or doing an hour of yoga. It requires a lot of self-discipline and is a means to attain a greater self-awareness – to recognize your own thoughts and inner self. That's also one of the reasons why it's useful for lucid dreaming because it enables you to get a better grasp of what is real (while awake) and the workings of your mind (while dreaming).

You can practise meditation by finding somewhere quiet where you won't be disturbed for a while. You can sit or lie down and it's best to close your eyes to avoid external visual stimuli. Soothing ambient music may help to get you in the mood, or you can opt to listen to a guided meditation, where the speaker talks you through the session and helps you to imagine being in a forest, floating on a lake, or any other relaxing activity in a serene location. The focus is initially on your breathing, not your thoughts, as you follow your breath on each inhale and exhale. If your mind wanders, which it probably will, just keep bringing your focus back to your breathing. The more you practise, the better you will become at it.

Eventually, this kind of focusing will help you to reach lucidity more easily as you learn to define the line between inner self-awareness and the outside world.

Lucid Dreaming vs. Meditation

Here are some interesting facts about meditation and lucid dreaming you might like to think about:

1. Meditators spend less time in REM sleep but have greater dream recall
2. Meditators have more lucid dreams
3. Both meditators and lucid dreamers display more field independence (which means they can separate details from the surrounding context)

When in a lucid state of dreaming, you can explore every aspect of your inner self. Although some might use it as a kind of home entertainment, during which they go jet-skiing or watch a sci-fi movie on demand, there is so much more to be gained from it than that. It can help you to solve problems, improve your performance, and guide you to resolve any issues that are troubling you. Imagine it is like entering the palace of your mind, filled with vast chambers containing wonderful treasures for you to explore. The possibilities are limitless.

If you want to go deeper and explore your spirituality, lucid dreaming can be developed into *dream yoga (or milam)*. This is an advanced Tibetan tantric practice to connect you with deeper aspects of your inner self and is aimed at self-transcendence. Here, you can go on a voyage of self-discovery using your dreams as a medium. As you learn to be more in control of your emotional state in dreams, you can also apply this to waking life, becoming happier, more contented, less stressed, and able to enjoy a greater sense of peace. Through dream yoga, you can use lucidity as a springboard in the real world, letting go of restrictions and feelings of being trapped by your circumstances. Sounds heavenly, doesn't it?

Dream yoga enables you to face your nightmares (or fears) and learn to see them for what they are, illusions of the mind. Once you realise this, you can use this insight in your waking world, understanding that fear really is a fictitious construct. As you wander through your nocturnal landscape, you can explore the expansiveness of your imagination and feel a real sense of being at one with the universe, without limits or worries. Now, who wouldn't want that?

Meditation, dream yoga and lucid dreaming make for perfect bed partners (a kind of oneiric love triangle, if you like…) and they are worth investigating. There's also something called sleep yoga, which has more to do with being aware during the REM stage of sleep but it's a very advanced meditation technique practised mainly by Tibetan Vajrayana Buddhist monks.

For most people, sleep is a chance to have as little awareness of what is going on around them as possible. For the lucid dreamer or sleep yogi, it's an opportunity to experience a mini epiphany in which the mind 'wakes up'. We can learn a lot about ourselves by exploring this inner space between dreams and reality, tap into undiscovered wisdom, and access parts of ourselves we didn't know existed.

Creating your own healing sanctuary

It's possible to enter a 'dream state' without being asleep at all, and this can be a chance to heal and restore your being. I do a lot of meditation and often 'journey' to my inner grove and visit my healing sanctuary. It's a place I've created in my mind that I access when I feel the need to destress, heal, rejuvenate my energy, and ground myself.

You can create your own healing sanctuary, depending on what appeals to you. As it's your sacred space, only accessible to you, you can make it however you like. Mine happens to be a round house, made of logs, deep in a woodland. There's an open hearth, and comfy rugs and furs lining the bed. It's warm, cosy, and smells of herbs and pine forests. Yours could be a little whitewashed house on a beach, a mountainside spa, a small boat on the lake, or even a garden full of fragrant flowers.

Whatever you decide, it can serve as your go-to place when you want to heal. Your mind can take you there whenever you wish, and you can stay there as long as you want.

Many cultures have the notion of a healing sanctuary where the participant moves from a conscious to a subconscious state. It may involve staring into the fire to see what images come up, watching the ocean waves or the stars twinkling at night. Druids tend to create theirs in a woodland grove because of the sacred power of trees and the compounds they emit into the surrounding air. Anyone who enjoys getting out into nature will know how rejuvenating it can be for mind and body and being at one with your surroundings is soul food for many people. But if you can't physically get to a particular location or specific place, you can create it in your mind.

Try it when you go to bed at night by conjuring up a place in your mind that feels right for you. Imagine you are there and notice how you feel: all the positive sensations of being safe, warm, protected and well. This is also a great way to begin practising the art of lucid dreaming.

Healing sanctuaries serve many purposes and can help you deal with both emotional and physical pain. They are a place to self-soothe and regain your balance when life gets you down. Whatever is going on in your job, relationships, or the world at large, it is possible to find a place of serenity and wellness and it begins within you.

Chapter 9

What's Next?

Reoccurring aspects within a dream

We can often find ourselves having the same dream over and over and wanting it to stop, but sometimes it might only be one aspect of a dream that reoccurs. Perhaps a particular piece of music is always playing, or we are consistently wearing the same outfit. It may be that no matter what the story or situation is in the dream, our condition within it stays the same.

In every dream I had for almost a 4-year period, I was partially paralysed from the waist down. My legs just wouldn't move at the same speed they do in real life. Every time I tried to run, they would behave as if being restricted in some way or weighed down. My dreams during these years were pure frustration – imagine how difficult being chased was, or trying to run towards the man of your dreams (quite literally) but instead of leaping across a sun-drenched meadow with the wind blowing through your hair and your billowing floaty dress, you drag your legs awkwardly behind you, looking like a slow-motion version of the hunchback of Notre Dame. Not quite the same experience. It got so bad towards the end of the 4 years that I was literally dragging myself along the floor whenever I needed to go anywhere in a dream.

I knew what was causing it; what was holding me back in my life, but for 4 years I was adamant I couldn't do anything about it. However, as soon as I started work on fixing it, my legs returned to normal in my dreams and I was once again able to complete a perfect Argentine Tango with any number of Strictly beefcakes.

Recurring dreams are very common, although it isn't until we begin to look at them that we can understand their importance. It's thought that we have them for a very good reason — to help us overcome unresolved conflicts in our waking lives. That being the case, they show us just how large a role dreams can play on our overall well-being and are not to be written off as pure figments of our imagination. They are scripts that can play over and over again on repeat for years, much like the sitcom 'Friends'.

You might be experiencing certain stress in your life or carrying issues around with you that you've been trying to ignore, which is why recurring dreams are your way out. If you have been seeing the same theme for a long time – even all your life – it's definitely worth looking into what that storyline is really saying.

There are some common themes, which also happen to be culturally linked. Your recurring dream of missing a flight, for instance, will be different to someone who has never seen an aeroplane, let alone travelled on one. What is common to these kinds of dreams is that they usually have negative content and make us feel strong emotions of fear, grief, anger, guilt, and so on. If you have a recurring dream of losing your teeth, that's not a pleasant experience, and neither is being chased or finding yourself locked in a room. But it's not the scenario itself that is important – it's those strong emotions that are evoked. They are what you need to pay attention to.

No one can tell you what your recurring dreams mean, but you can pinpoint those emotions and try to see where they are coming from. Anger, guilt and fear are all normal human reactions to stressful or worrying situations. Perhaps you feel stressed in real life, or insecure, frustrated, confused...think about it.

Your brain is a great regulator of emotions, and it likes to keep everything shipshape so when you have issues that need sorting out, your brain finds ways to bring your attention to them. It's like having to remove barnacles from the bottom of a boat to help maintain speed and efficiency... you have to dive underwater and scrape them off. In the same way, having a recurring dream about falling, or being unable to move is your brain's way of trying to process a difficult situation or painful event.

Dreaming about drowning over and over again doesn't necessarily mean that you are genuinely worried about that happening. It could be more of a metaphor that represents feelings of being powerless or helpless in real life. Maybe you feel overwhelmed with your daily responsibilities, are unable to change your circumstances, worried about your business failing or any number of other things. When you think about it in that context, you will begin to unravel what's on your mind and then you are in a much better position to do something about it.

These recurring dreams might be disturbing, but they aren't the same as nightmares in which you might relive past traumas. That's something different and could be a sign of post-traumatic stress disorder, for which you should seek professional help. Recurring dreams aren't usually connected to a real-life event but are more linked to some kind of emotion that you need to work through such as shame, frustration, anger, and so on. Think of them as reading a story or fable that has some underlying message or meaning that you just need to abstract, and you'll get what I mean.

If you see the same person in your recurring dreams or the repetition of certain objects/events, this is also an attempt by your brain to resolve your emotional concerns. For example, you might keep seeing your child, parent, friend, or lover on repeat, albeit in different situations. It's worth concentrating on your relationship with that person and considering:

1. Is it a strong relationship?
2. Is there any conflict there?
3. Are there any unresolved issues between you?
4. Are they under your care?

5. Do you miss them, for whatever reason?

Once you get the ball rolling, you will gain insight into why this character keeps appearing and that can help you to strengthen, heal, or balance the relationship you have with them in real life. Maybe you are overprotective about them or too emotionally/financially/socially attached for your own good. Perhaps you want to have more contact with them or need to create more distance. There are an infinite number of things that are playing out in your dreams, but you are the only one who can find out what is bothering you.

Or maybe, like me, these people don't represent themselves at all, but rather a characteristic, one of your own characteristics that needs attention.

Filtering your recurring dreams

I can't ignore the fact that some of the things we dream about often are just hard-wired into our physiology. A mother dreaming about her children being in danger is a natural response… like an evolutionary mechanism that provides the brain with the opportunity to practise escaping predators or being more aware of dangers.

If you often dream about your teeth falling out, it may have more to do with you clenching your teeth during sleep rather than signifying something more ominous. As a one-time teeth clencher, I can say that it was a habit I also did during the day when I felt stressed. It wasn't until I resolved what was making me feel so anxious that I stopped the teeth-clenching (and dreams of losing teeth) in my sleep, too.

It's also possible that constantly dreaming of looking for a toilet may mean that you regularly need to urinate at night. Dreaming of being naked in public could be because you feel cold in bed and need to wear something warmer. Obviously, if you keep having these dreams even though you don't need to go to the toilet or feel cold, then there could be something more there that you need to investigate.

The best way to process recurring dreams is to write them down or visualise them when you wake up and then decode them. If they still persist, try changing the ending in your narrative to something more pleasant. You can also try lucid dreaming, which I talked about in the previous chapter. This gives you control over what you will dream about and how to act within the dream scenario, ultimately liberating you from that ongoing cycle.

There are other strategies you can try to avoid having unpleasant recurring dreams, although it's good to think about what they may be trying to tell you in the first place. If they are becoming too upsetting and disrupting your sleep or making it difficult for you to cope while awake during the day, you could:

A. Talk to a health professional, who may advise counselling or therapy. You might gain a lot of personal insight from this course of action and be able to work through whatever is bothering you.

B. Do regular exercise to get rid of pent-up stress and improve your physical condition. It may also make you so tired that you sleep a lot sounder each night.

C. Try some relaxation exercises before you go to bed. You can practise meditation, breathing exercises, guided visualisations, or just sit quietly for ten minutes before going to sleep.

D. Avoid watching TV or scrolling through your social media when you do go to lie down because this just makes your brain overstimulated and that's the last thing you need for a good night's sleep.

E. Talk to someone you trust about your dreams. This will help you to put them into perspective and notice anything useful in reference to your waking life. It may simply highlight some concerns that you hadn't paid much attention to until now, which can be quite revealing.

F. Follow a regular sleep routine, going to bed roughly the same time each night, and waking up around about the same time each morning. This can help you to fall asleep easier and allow your brain to do what it does best in full alignment with your circadian clock.

Dreams and the future

Can dreams really predict the future? That depends on who you talk to. While there's no hard scientific evidence to support the claim as of yet, no doubt you've heard plenty of examples where someone saw an event or incident in their dreams that came true a few days later. Abraham Lincoln, for example, reportedly told his friend Ward Hill Lamon of how he dreamt about his own assassination and Carl Jung wrote about predicting his own mother's death[23]. Maybe someone predicted a plane crash that actually happened or foresaw the

---

[23] C.G. Jung., Memories, Dream, Reflections, Vintage, 1989

assassination of the Pope... coincidence or not?

You might also have heard people say that they had a bad dream about someone, which led them to feel worried when they woke up, only to see their fears being confirmed soon thereafter. For instance, a woman dreams that her mother is sick. The next day, she rushes to her mother's home, only to find her unconscious on the floor and in urgent need of medical treatment.

What's the truth behind this kind of occurrence and does it matter?

If you have ever had a dream that turned out to come true in the future, you are not alone. Many people have experienced the same thing at some point in their lives, proving it's a common phenomenon that has aroused the interest of the brain boffins. When scientists do discuss this type of brain activity, they talk about *precognitive dreams*. In layman's terms, this simply means any dreams that give you information about the future you wouldn't otherwise have. It doesn't sound very scientific, if you think about it.

Brazilian neuroscientist Sidarta Ribeiro put forward the idea that dreams may have a predictive function in his book *The Oracle of the Night: The History and Science of Dreams*. After much research, he came to the conclusion that although dreams may not exactly be like an oracle, they could work as a sophisticated computer that simulates possible future outcomes based on what has happened up till now. If your dreams help you to consolidate memories and create new ideas, then it's possible that what you see in them will predict a certain outcome in the future.

There's also something called *selective recall*, which is when an incident in your waking life seems to parallel a dream event, making you more likely to notice the similarities. If for example you dream of a pig, and the next day you see something on TV about pig farming, it doesn't mean you predicted anything about pigs, but it does make you refer to your dream and create a connection in your mind.

If you do believe that your dreams can predict the future, that's fine. It's your personal choice, as long as it doesn't lead you to rely too much on dreams as some kind of crystal ball for everything you do in life. The future holds such infinite possibilities that it's impossible to know what is going to happen next and worrying about it will leave you feeling anxious and fearful. If something does occur in real life that you predicted in your dreams, it might make you take more notice of further dreams, although not every one will be an omen of things to come.

Your subconscious stores all the information you need in life and, as you dream, it can bring up certain things that you don't normally think about. When it manifests something like a break-up with a partner in a dream, it's because you have internalised thoughts and feelings that your conscious hasn't processed properly. Your dreams are the canvas on which everything is played out and if, for example, you dream of having an awful row with your partner and then break up the next day, it's more likely that you had unresolved issues anyway, such as feeling insecure in the relationship or unhappy. Did the dream predict the break-up or bring unresolved emotions to the surface?

Scientific research doesn't have answers to these questions yet and although some explanations sound plausible, we still don't understand the full role of dreams. Personally, I'm excited to see what scientific developments come up in the future! In the meantime, who's to say that those cultures relying on dreams for spiritual guidance and wisdom about future events have got it wrong?

Thoughts to ponder

- People who have been blind from birth have dreams formed from other senses, including touch, smell, and sound.

- Elephants sleep standing up during non-REM sleep (but lie down for REM sleep).
- Marsupials do not experience REM sleep at all (kangaroos don't dream!).
- During a lifetime, the average person spends about six years dreaming.
- When trees shut down for winter, do they dream?
- The most common word uttered while sleep talking is *No*!
- Einstein's insights about the speed of light and the principle of relativity came to him after having a vivid dream.
- Google has developed a vision software called DeepDream to investigate artificial neural networks and their potential to dream.

The mind boggles!

Time to dream

Now that you have come to the end of this book, you are ready to begin the intriguing journey of interpreting your dreams.

★ You can start by getting a nice journal – one that will inspire you to use it. Some dream journals or diaries available for purchase have prompts in them to help you record various bits of information. If that seems useful, go for it, but you can also buy any blank notebook where you can draw whatever comes to mind when recording your dream. Take your journal with you when you go out in case you remember something related to your dream that you want to note down.

★ Remember the **DREAM** prompts: **D**etails, **R**epresentatives, **E**nvironment, **A**ctions, & **M**oment in Time to guide you.

★ Highlight any key elements or words in your notes, such as objects, people, colours, feelings and actions.

Notice any recurring patterns and consider what each highlighted word means to you.

★ Once you get used to recording the details of your dreams, look for common elements that occur across several dreams. By noticing them, you will gradually be able to decode their purpose and understand how they relate to your life.

★ If you remember some of your recurring dreams, sit down and go over them, noting any themes, people, objects, or feelings that seem to be most prominent. Take the time to reflect on them, without feeling the need to force an explanation. It will come to you in time.

★ Try some meditation before you go to bed. Even ten minutes of deep relaxation can help to open up your mind and clear any clutter accumulated throughout the day.

Troubleshooting

People who have read this book are always asking me, "What if an aspect of my dreams has multiple meanings to me? How do I know which is the right one?"

It's not an easy question to answer, simply because everyone is different, and the process is so personal. But what I have found works is to read through my transcript again right before I go to sleep. Often, this is enough to put me back into the same dream scenario. I then see if I can pick up any more details or see if the dream takes a different turn.

Rest assured: if the message is important enough, your subconscious will find a way to make it clearer for you!

Conclusion

*"We make realities out of our dreams
and dreams out of our realities. We
are the dreamers of the dream."*
– Roald Dahl

Dreams are part of our human experience.
They have shaped great civilizations,
inspired works of art, warned of impending
catastrophes and forged powerful empires.
They have become intrinsic to certain
cultures, played a vital role in emotional
healing, and exposed our state of mind.
They are, in effect, indispensable.

This book is my contribution to the subject
of dreams and their interpretation, which I
believe can be truly liberating and
empowering. Throughout my life, I've been
fascinated by the topic and I'm now at the
point where I'm fully convinced of its
usefulness. My dreams have helped me to
work through problems, find solutions, and
grow both emotionally and spiritually.

Although the neuroscientists are still trying to form a consolidated theory about why we dream and what they can offer us, I often think of it the other way around:

What if we never experienced dreams while sleeping?

Can you imagine sleep without dreams? How would that be? What effect would it have on your waking state?

If the world of dreams allows you to consolidate information, create new memories, sort through your emotions and nurture creativity, all of which we know are essential for our cognitive functioning, how would you function in a dreamless life?

For me, dreams play an essential role in our well-being, and they hold the key to all of our internal worries, doubts, fears, hopes, illusions, and realities. They act like a highly sophisticated conveyor belt that sorts, colour-codes, wraps, and stores emotions. When they come across an imperfect, oddly shaped piece of information, they point it out to you and say, "What do you want me to do with this?" The onus is on you to decide. If you keep throwing it back in without examining it, it's eventually going to clog up the whole system.

You are the engineer of your dreams and it's you who can examine each piece of information to determine its usefulness.

You can ask yourself:

Does it require more processing?
Does it have something important to tell you?
Do you still need it?

In this book, I've talked about the importance of sleep from a physiological point of view, and gone over the cycles of sleep that are so crucial to our health.

We've looked at how sleep restores our immune system, regulates our hormones, and even replenishes cancer-fighting cells. We also saw how sleep is the time when our brain decodes data and creates long-term memories, allowing it to reboot so we can function effectively the next day.

All of these vital processes need dreams if they are to be successful. Dreams are the playground for the subconscious to explore and discover. If our waking state is the classroom where we are expected to sit, listen, and learn, dreams are the schoolyard where we can run around, interact, and experience freedom from restraints. We certainly need that if we want to grow and develop a healthy sense of self.

Dreams can be strange, bizarre, weird, fantastical, freaky, grotesque, odd, surreal, peculiar, outlandish, and plain ridiculous. They can be puzzling, disturbing, scary, confusing and even embarrassing but they are an integral part of who we are. Freud and Jung, who we met earlier on in the book, had some great insights into the psychological implications of our dreams. Their ideas about the subconscious mind, the psyche, taboos and more, helped dreams to be taken more seriously by the scientific community. Today, whole university departments and laboratories are dedicated to the social, neurological, and physiological study of dreams, which is quite impressive, considering.

As a society, we may not pay that much attention to our dreams anymore, although many cultures around the world still see them as a mirror reflection of the waking state. They are talked about, shared amongst one another, and seen as portals into the spiritual realm of whole communities. Dreams are paths to healing for both the individual and the group, as well as acting as a link between the living and the ancestral line. They are viewed as sources of great wisdom and cultural identity, offering insights into everything from the best hunting spots to cures for sickness and disease.

You won't find any dream dictionaries in the pockets of a Native American and there is no list in alphabetical order of what this or that means. Everything is part of one big dream and different realms can be accessed and astral planes crossed, especially if one is skilled in this tradition. For many indigenous peoples today, dreams are still extremely important aspects of life, so why not for us?

I hope you try the 5-step process for interpreting your dreams that I have presented here, using the DREAM prompts that have become an invaluable tool for me. The beauty of the process is that anyone can do it and it doesn't take too much time or effort. Before you know it, it will be opening up a world of new possibilities; a world in which your inner emotions and thoughts can be deciphered to help you reach your full potential.

Learning to control your dreams may sound like science fiction, but it is possible to master that practice through lucid dreaming and meditation. As we learn more about the brain's function and the sleep cycle, we are getting nearer to understanding the mechanics of lucid dreaming and how we can play a more active role in that.

Imagine being able to tune into your dreams at will – no matter where you are – by learning how to direct your mind through quiet contemplation and meditation. Imagine being able to change the negative loop of recurring dreams and nightmares into something more therapeutic and positive. Wouldn't that be something!

Your mind is a glorious city of glittering towers, shimmering palaces, and sacred temples. As you dream, you have the chance to wander around every street and unlock every door. By learning how to follow your emotional map, you can discover a rich array of treasures that will bring clarity and meaning into your life.

Through dream interpretation, you can free yourself of worries and fears, create new pathways for self-development, and even tap into your creative abilities.

There is so much to be gained from this exploration of your innermost self and I hope I have inspired you to look closer and discover more.

Until then, keep dreaming!

Acknowledgments

Mother nature is such a guiding light in my life. Providing inspiration and influence over all that I am and all that I do, but there are a few key people who have also helped me to realise along the way that firstly, **knowledge is for sharing** (The legendary Bruce Lawson, my Trails Guide Instructor at EcoTraining South Africa) and secondly, that **education is a gift** - one that can never be taken away from you or stolen. The attitude and humility of African people reminds me of this every time I spend time with them. Zikomo!

To all those who have given me the confidence to overcome the dreaded "imposter syndrome" and put this book out there; I am so very grateful to have you in my life. I hope this book helps others on their journey towards becoming better versions of themselves in the same way these people have done for me. Our minds are the storehouse of wisdom, and we must keep topping them up.

About The Author

Raised on a dairy farm at the foot of the South Downs in Sussex, England, Joanne has always had a deep fascination with all things natural, wild,and unexplored.

After a 25-year career in manufacturing software that took her all over the world, Joanne was able to quit the "rat race" and follow her passion for nature.

Now a qualified safari field guide and seasonal manager of a luxury bush camp in Zambia, Joanne loves nothing more than spending time in wild places with her binoculars and sharing stories around the campfire.

When she's not guiding guests on safari, Joanne spends her free time restoring and rewilding a small piece of woodland near her home in Mid-Sussex.

Sources/Further Reading

Hirshkowitz, Max et al. "National Sleep Foundation's sleep time duration recommendations: methodology and results summary." *Sleep health* vol. 1,1 (2015)

Natural Sleep and Its Seasonal Variations in Three Pre-industrial Societies, Current Biology Vol. 25, Issue 21 (2015)

Shakespeare, W., Hamlet, Act 3, Scene 1, Amazon Classics (2017)

Walker, M. P., Why We Sleep, Penguin (2018)

Loftus, E F, and M R Klinger. "Is the Unconscious Smart or Dumb?." *The American psychologist* vol. 47,6 (1992)

https://www.ted.com/talks/matt_walker_the_sur prising_health_benefits_of_dreaming

Kahn, D., Stickgold, R., Pace-Schott, E.F. and Hobson, J.A.,Dreaming and waking consciousness: a character recognition study. Journal of Sleep Research, 9: 317-325. (2000)

Schredl, Michael et al. Typical dreams: stability and gender differences. *The Journal of psychology* vol. 138,6 (2004)

Hobson, J. A., The Dreaming Brain: How the Brain Creates Both the Sense and the Nonsense of Dreams, Basic books (1988)

Nicolas Deperrois, Mihai A Petrovici, Walter Senn, Jakob Jordan, Learning cortical representations through perturbed and adversarial dreaming *eLife* (2022)

The Complete Works of Chuang Tzu, Columbia University Press (1968)

Chaucer, G. Canterbury Tales, Xist Classics (2015)

Guillaume de Lorris, The Romance of the Rose. Oxford World's Classics (2009)

The Pearl, (Anonymous) (2021)

Pizan, Christine, The Book of the City of Ladies. Penguin (1999)

The Collected Major Works of Sir Thomas Browne (Collection Includes Notes and Letters on the Natural History of Norfolk, Religio Medici, And More) (2017)

Freud, S., The Interpretation of Dreams: The Complete Definitive Text, Basic Books (2010)

Aserinsky, E. & Kleitman, N., Regularly Occurring Periods of Eye Motility, and Concomitant Phenomena, During Sleep, Science Journal (1953)

Jung, C. G., Instinct and the Unconscious, British Journal of Psychology (1919)

Best Practice Guide for the Treatment of Nightmare Disorder in Adults Standards of Practice Committee, R. Nisha Aurora, M.D., et al. (2010)

Kopenawa, D., The Falling Sky: Words of a Yanomami Shaman, Belknap Press (2013)

Faraday, A., The Dream Game, Harper & Row (1990)

https://news.wisc.edu/meditation-produces-positive-changes-in-the-brain/

Dickens, C. Oliver Twist, Penguin Classics (2003)

Julian Mutz, Amir-Homayoun Javadi, Exploring the neural correlates of dream phenomenology and altered states of consciousness during sleep, *Neuroscience of Consciousness*, Volume 2017, Issue 1 (2017)

Dali, S., 50 Secrets of Magic Craftsmanship, Dover Fine Art, History of Art (1992)

C.G. Jung., Memories, Dream, Reflections, Vintage, 1989

Ribeiro, S., The Oracle of the Night: The History and Science of Dreams, Bantam Press (2021)

Printed in Great Britain
by Amazon

20657976R00129